GW00372391

THE BIG HAIRY ALMANACKERS 2009

SINCE 1979

RARE PLUMS FROM THE ARCHIVE

Big Hairy Almanackers 2009

Copyright Dennis Publishing/Fulchester Industries.

Written, drawn and produced by Graham Dury,
~~Davy Jones~~ and Simon Thorp.
Additional material: Alex Collier, Chris Donald,
Simon Donald, Simon Ecob and Lew Stringer.
Design: Wayne Histon-Gamble.
Production: Stevie Glover.

Viz is published ten times a year by Dennis Publishing, 30 Cleveland
Street, London W1T 4JD. To subscribe, call 0844 844 0380.

www.viz.co.uk

Printed December 2008. Pulped January 2009

CONTENTS

THE BIG HAIRY ALMANACKERS 2009

HERE at SexistMatch, it's our dream to help you to meet the bird of your dreams. All you have to do is complete our simple survey. It'll only take a few minutes - you could do it now, while you're sitting on the toilet. Whatever sort of relationship you are looking for, whether it's a lifelong companion to hoover round you and make your tea, or just a hurried knee trembler in a taxi queue, you are sure to find your ideal piece from amongst our thousands of members.

Questionnaire

Please complete in block capitals

1. Your details

Mr ❑ Surname: _____

First name: _____ Address: _____

_____

Post code: _____ Tel: _____

I am seriously interested in making my life easier by sorting myself out with a bird. Signed _____

2. Personal Information

Status: Single ❑ Living with mam ❑ Tramp ❑

Age: 18-40 ❑ 41-42 ❑ over 42 ❑

Occupation: Employed ❑ Dole ❑ Criminal ❑ Coma ❑

Religion: None ❑

Height: 5'2" ❑ Other ❑

Beer gut: Six Pack ❑ Party Seven ❑ Watney's Red Barrel ❑

How long do you spend on the toilet?: 2-3 hrs ❑ 3-4 hrs ❑ Over 4 hrs ❑

3. Education

School: Comprehensive ❑ Borstal ❑

Qualifications: O Levels ❑ Cycling Proficiency ❑ TV Licence ❑

4. Your personality

(Tick which traits closely describe you)

❑ Aggressive   ❑ Opinionated
❑ Lecherous   ❑ Belligerent
❑ Argumentative   ❑ Misogynistic
❑ Nasty   ❑ Lazy
❑ Alcoholic   ❑ Stupid

5. Points of View

(Tick any statements which describe your attitudes)

❑ I believe a woman's place is in the home

❑ I'd rather go to the pub than have a romantic night in.

❑ A man's best friend is his mother.

❑ I'd rather go to the pub than go shopping on Saturday morning.

❑ I don't know how to boil an egg, and what's more I'm proud of it.

❑ I want my tea on the table when I get in.

❑ I'd rather go to the pub than do the washing up.

❑ Shut up, I'm trying to watch this.

❑ I'd rather go to the pub than anything.

❑ I've never done it with a lady.

6. Tick any of these pictures that interest you.

 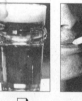

❑   ❑   ❑

7. Hobbies and Interests

(Tick any of the subjects that interest you)

❑ Masturbating   ❑ Beer
❑ Lager   ❑ Fags
❑ Curry   ❑ Tits
❑ Farting   ❑ Women's arses
❑ Hard core porn   ❑ Watching telly
❑ Lying down   ❑ Gambling
❑ Going for a shit   ❑ Eating your tea
❑ Swearing   ❑ Fannies

8. Reading material

(Tick which of the following you like to read)

❑ Razzle
❑ Escort
❑ Freeman's Catalogue bra pages
❑ Sunday Sport
❑ Pages 183-186 of 'The Rats' by James Herbert

9. The kind of bird you are after

Minimum age: maximum age:

Tits: Large ❑ Huge ❑ Fucking massive ❑ Comical ❑

Marital status: Single ❑ Divorced ❑ Hubby inside ❑ Hubby on oil rigs ❑

Easyness: Easy ❑ Slack ❑ Dead cert ❑ Clown's pocket ❑

FINBARR'S GRAND DOUBLE ENTENDRE SEARCH

FINBARR IS ON HIS WAY TO HIS LOCAL NEWSAGENT TO BUY THE VIZ HAIRY ALMANACKERS 2009, BUT UNFORTUNATELY, HE'S SO EXCITED AT THE PROSPECT OF GETTING HIS HANDS ON HIS FAVOURITE COMIC THAT HE HASN'T NOTICED SEVERAL DOUBLE ENTENDRES TAKING PLACE AROUND HIM ON THE STREET. WE RECKON THAT AT LEAST 100 CHEAP SEXUAL INNUENDOS AND PROFANISAURUS TERMS ARE DEPICTED IN THIS ACTION-PACKED SCENE, BUT HOW MANY CAN **YOU** SPOT?

THE BAT SLAGS

HA! I, THE *POKER*, ARCH VILLAIN. - AND MY FIENDISH *SHAGGING GAS* - STRIKE ONCE AGAIN!

EMPTY THE SAFE, MEN - AND REMEMBER... DO **NOT** TAKE OFF YOUR GAS MASKS!

MEANWHILE, ON THE OTHER SIDE OF GOTHCHESTER...

... SO I SAYS TO 'IM I SAYS, RIGHT, I'LL SUCK YER OFF, BURRIM NOT GOIN' T' SWALLOW, COS' YER'VE GORRA BOIL ON YER LID...

THE MOUSE & ANCHOR A WITNEYS HOUSE

..'AN IF IT BUSTS IN ME GOB, I'LL PROBLY SPEW UP IN YER UNDERKEX - AN' THEY'LL NOT LET YER BACK IN THE 'OSTEL.

NA-AA-AA!

AYUP TRAY... LOOK!

COME ON SAN- TO THE SLAG-CAVE!

'OLD ON. I'LL 'AVE TO GO FOR A PISS FIRST.

SHORTLY...

SLOW DOWN, TRAY. I'VE BROKE ONE OF ME 'EELS.

WHIRRR!

HONK!

SLAG POL

OW! ME FANNY!

WHUMP!

OOYAH!

CHRIST! ME FUCKIN' ARSE!

WHY CAN'T WE USE THE FRIGGIN' STAIRS, BAT-SLAG?

SHUT YER FUCKIN' RATTLE, KNOBIN, AN' GET THE SLAGMOBILE STARTED.

IT'S NOT FAIR, BAT-SLAG. WHY'S IT ALWAYS ME WHAT'S GORRA DRIVE?

I TOLD YER. I'VE 'AD A SKINFUL. I'VE BIN ON SNAKEBITES SINCE DINNERTIME YOU'VE ONLY 'AD LAGER.

'ERE. WHAT'S YOUR KNICKERS DOIN' IN THE ASHTRAY?

PLEASE KEEP CLEAR BATT- CAVE EXITIN CONSTANT US

CLANG!

THEY'RE NOT MINE - THEY'RE YOURS. LOOK AT THE SKIDS.

OH AYE.

I'VE BIN LOOKIN' FOR THEM EVERYWHERE. I MUST OF LEFT 'EM THERE WHEN THAT TROLLEY PARK ATTENDANT AT SAFEWAYS FUCKED US BEHIND THE BOTTLE BANK. YOU KNOW - 'IM WI' THE DEAF AID AN' THE CLUB FOOT...LOST AN EYE IN THE FIRST WORLD WAR...

OH, 'IM. I THINK I GIVE 'IM A WANK ONCE AT THE PICTURES.

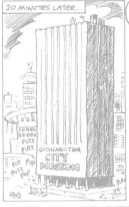

Why trains are LATE

Whenever we go to a railway station to catch a train, our train is always late. Sometimes trains do not arrive at all, and instead we must catch a bus or taxi to get us to our destination. Invariably we are late, for work perhaps, or for an important meeting. Let's take a look behind the scenes of Britain's busy railways and discover how exactly trains are late.

* A train's busy day begins at the train shed where mechanics inspect it, fill it with fuel and prepare it for a hard day's work. This train won't be going anywhere today. It is already late because its driver is at home in bed. He had got "backache". The passengers waiting at the station are told that their train is cancelled due to 'staff shortages'.

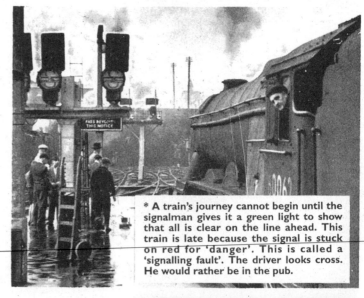

* A train's journey cannot begin until the signalman gives it a green light to show that all is clear on the line ahead. This train is late because the signal is stuck on red for 'danger'. This is called a 'signalling fault'. The driver looks cross. He would rather be in the pub.

* Signals are not the only faulty things on our railways. Here a set of points have frozen. An old man tries to mend them with an outdated piece of equipment. Despite his efforts, 'frozen points' cause many trains to be late.

* In winter 'snow' causes trains to be late. Nowadays trains are fitted with expensive snow blowing equipment and snow ploughs to clear the track. But these only work on certain types of snow. This train is over 4 hours late due to 'the wrong type of snow'.

In summer hot weather causes trains to be late. The heat from the sun buckles the metal tracks.

* Now it is autumn, and this diesel train hurries through the wind on the way to pick up its passengers. They wait eagerly on the platform a few miles up the line. The train is due any moment, but little do they know it won't arrive for another two hours at least. This is because leaves have fallen onto the track, and they cause its wheels to slip.

The passengers on the platform begin to get angry when their train does not arrive. Meanwhile, passengers on the following train, and on several trains behind that, are also getting angry. Their trains are all running late.

* This train is late because it is old. It is unreliable and keeps breaking down. It should have been replaced several years ago.

* This train is late because it is new. New, modern trains often have basic design faults which cause them to break down. These are known as 'minor teething troubles'.

Continued over...

*Here our driver is ringing up the signalman. He wonders why his train has been stopped for over an hour at a red signal. In the signal box, one hundred and fifty miles up ahead, flashing lights on his hi-technology display tell the over-worked signalman that his equipment has broken down due to lack of maintenance. He tells the driver he has no idea when his train will be able to go.

* The train crew spring into action. The driver tells the Senior Conductor that the train is stuck, and he makes an unprofessional announcement on the train's public address system. His accent is barely discernable to the majority of passengers. Consequently they do not hear his feeble apology, or the totally inadequate explanation he gives for the delay. A similar announcement is made by a disinterested sounding woman over a hopelessly inadequate public address system in the station, for the benefit of the passengers who are now scowling angrily at the train information board, and vowing never to use the train ever again. They cannot decipher her muffled, inaudible voice.

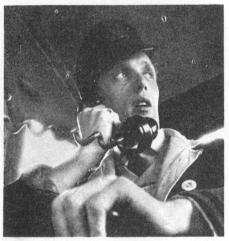

* Meanwhile back on the train the buffet should be doing a roaring trade in refreshments with their captive market of starving passengers. But the buffet is quiet, and the steward, who is normally being abrupt, (to the point of rudeness) with customers, is standing idle. This is because on a 500 mile journey from Torquay to Edinburgh, the buffet ran out of teas, coffees, hot and cold snacks, etc. at Bristol. All they have left are salted peanuts, and one slice of carrot cake with lemon icing on top.

* Back at the station another unsuspecting passenger pays a bloody fortune for a ticket. She does not know it, but her train is already 5 hours late.

Biffa Bacon's Camping Capers

By Dudley Chuckles

FIRST PUBLISHED IN "Viz Comic Funnies" AUGUST 1964

peer pressured

The Magazine that would have you believe £100 vests are the most important thing in the world.

SEPTEMBER 1999 £2.80

SOME ACTRESS

in her underwear: and it looks like you can see pubes through her pants.

100 'MUST HAVE' ALUMINIUM GIZMOS YOU DON'T NEED AND CAN'T AFFORD.

SOME OTHER ACTRESS

in a swimsuit.

No pubes, but a definite camel's foot.

The demographic analysis department of the vast publishing corporation that owns this title ordered us to write

BEER, FOOTIE & BIRDS

just here on the cover 'hot spot'

The WHOLE WORLD is wearing Ermenegildo Zegna suits - and you buy your clothes at Milletts.

PLUS
AN ARTICLE WHICH CASUALLY SUGGESTS THAT EVERYONE HAS SLEPT WITH LOADS MORE WOMEN THAN YOU HAVE.

FOR lads... ABOUT lads... BY graduate media twats contractually obliged to follow the diktats of a 'focus group'.

OUT NOW!

21

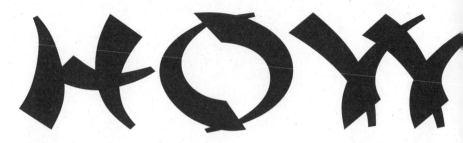

HOYY

THE ANCIENT Martial Arts of the world all have their own unique histories, forms and techniques. The noble North-eastern art of *How Yee* (literally meaning 'Excuse me') has its roots in rough street fighting, but has over the centuries been refined into a powerful technique for rough fighting in pubs, clubs, chip shops and amusement arcades. Acknowledged master of the

Move 1 — TEK THIS

The simplest of all *How Yee* moves. A sharp, straight punch in the gob thrown with the aggressor's leading hand, swiftly followed by a second attack (see 2.)

Move 2 — AN' THIS

A powerful straight punch to the nose or gob with the aggressor's rear hand. Usually thrown immediately after the *Tek This*, and together the moves are known as *Tek This... An' This*.

Move 5 — POD BORSTAH

Here, Master Grandfatha enlists the help of another pupil, Fatha. The challenger is supported under the arms and behind the head. The *How Yee* practitioner then delivers a series of toe-end punts to his opponent's nuts, effectively incapacitating him and preventing him from spilling any more pints.

Move 6 — WAALL STOTTAH

Even after the *Pod Borstah*, a tenacious opponent may still be capable of looking at you funny. To counter this, the skilled exponent of *How Yee* would execute this move. Using simultaneous thrusting movements, the offender's head is repeatedly twatted against a hard, vertical surface such as a brick wall, lamp post or pillar box.

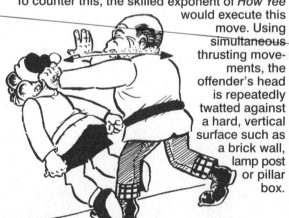

Eastern Art of Unprovoked Aggression

art, Grandfatha Bacon demonstrates a few of the most commonly used manoeuvres on his pupil, Biffhoppah.

Warning: The following moves are very powerful and potentially dangerous. The true master of How Yee would resort to their use only after extremely slight provocation, such as somebody looking at him funny, accidentally brushing against him in a crouded pub, or not being a Geordie.

Move 3 — CHIN YEE

An effective punch, powerfully delivered up and under the jaw, resulting in the transgressor being lifted six inches vertically. Can be delivered whilst holding a pint glass or a bunch of keys.

Move 4 — HEED STOMP

In *How Yee*, very little energy is needed to incapacitate an opponent by delivering a *Heed Stomp*. The knee of either leg, or for the experienced fighter, both legs together are raised to waist height before the heel of the boot is brought down with pinpoint accuracy onto the opponent's head.

Move 7 — THE CHAIR

Like Karate, *How Yee* is essentially a weaponless fighting system. However, certain moves may require the use of everyday objects. Here, Master Grandfatha uses the chair as an extension of his own arms to conclude an engagement swiftly and with the maximum of unpleasantness.

Move 8 — THE TELLY

Although unconscious on the floor, there is still a risk that the transgressor is not a Geordie. In *How Yee*, relative size of the combatants is not as important as one might think. At a mere 5' 4", Master Grandfatha demonstrates how he uses the weight of a 32" television set against his opponent, bringing the bout to a swift conclusion.

FROM COW TO DOORSTEP
The Miracle of Milk

The wholesome pinta packed with vitamins and goodness begins its incredible journey in a field in the English countryside. Here cows eat grass which goes into their udders where, by miracle of nature, it is turned into milk.

The milk maid milks the cow to remove the milk, cream, butter and cheese. And yoghurt. At the dairy the milk is put in milk bottles and topped up with cream before the silver foil lids are carefully glued into place.

It's 5.30am and most of us are still asleep as the milkman makes his rounds.

It's 7.30 and time for breakfast. All over Britain millions of school children start their day with a favourite treat – milk! Who'd have thought that only three hours earlier the milk you are pouring onto your cornflakes was a clump of grass in Mother Nature's field.

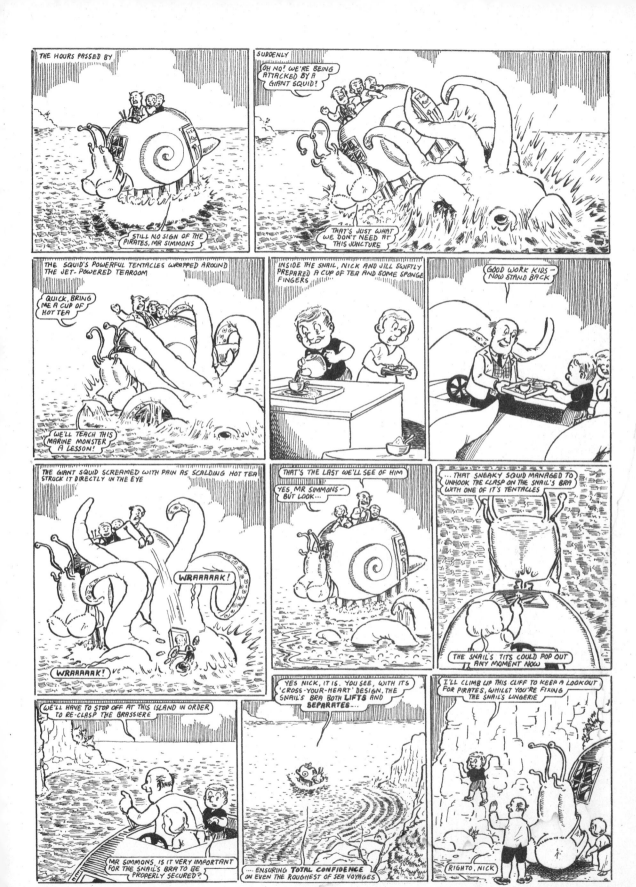

BUT WHEN HE REACHED THE TOP OF THE CLIFF, NICK RECEIVED THE SHOCK OF HIS LIFE

CRUMBS! THE PIRATE SHIP IS MOORED IN THE VERY NEXT COVE

THIS MUST BE THE ISLAND WHERE QUEEN VICTORIA BURIED THE CROWN JEWELS

NICK'S BLOOD RAN COLD AS HE HEARD THE CAPTAIN'S GRUFF VOICE ECHO AROUND THE BAY

AH-HAR, MY HEARTIES! IN A FEW HOURS THE CROWN JEWELS WILL BE MINE!

YO HO HO, AND A PIECE OF EIGHT

AND UNDER ENGLISH LAW, WHOEVER OWNS THE CROWN JEWELS AUTOMATICALLY SUCCEEDS TO THE THRONE

SO THAT MEANS THAT I, CAPTAIN DEATHBEARD, WILL SOON BECOME THE NEW KING OF ENGLAND! AH-HAR, AH-HAR!

YOU TWO STAY AND GUARD QUEEN VICTORIA WHILE THE REST OF US GO AND DIG UP THOSE JEWELS

AYE-AYE, CAP'N

THE YOUNG BOY HURRIED BACK TO TELL THE OTHERS WHAT HE HAD SEEN AND HEARD

IF WE TAKE THOSE TWO GUARDS BY SURPRISE WE SHOULD BE ABLE TO OVERPOWER THEM AND TAKE CONTROL OF THE SHIP

LET'S JUST HOPE THE OTHER PIRATES DON'T RETURN TOO SOON

AND SO

IS EVERYONE READY?

YES, MR SIMMONS

THEN LET'S GO!

WHOOSH! WITH A BLAST FROM IT'S JET ENGINES THE MIGHTY BIG-BOOBED TEAROOM SWOOPED DOWN ON THE PIRATE SHIP

THE TWO BEWILDERED GUARDS WERE SOON ON THE DEFENSIVE

BUT MEANWHILE ON THE ISLAND

HERE ARE THE CROWN JEWELS, CAP'N

EXCELLENT! LET US RETURN TO THE SHIP WHERE I SHALL BE MADE KING

ZOUNDS! OUR SHIP IS BEING ATTACKED BY A LARGE JET-POWERED HOVERING SNAIL...

...WITH BIG TITS

FORWARD, ME HEARTIES!!

29

FUN & GAMES
with
Roger Mellie

The fondest memories I have of my days at Fulchester Boarding School for Well Off Boys are the games my chums and I would always play together. Here's just a few. I hope you enjoy playing them as much as I did (and still do!)

Swearing with Matches

This is a spiffing way to pass the time behind the bicycle sheds inbetween puffs on a cigarette. All you need to play it are eleven matchsticks. See how I've cleverly arranged them into a rude word – 'TWAT'. See how many other swear words you can make by re-arranging the same eleven matches, then compare your results with my answers below.

The Milk Race

This is a game to play with your chums after lights out in the dorm. And you don't need a bicycle. All you need is a dirty magazine and a box of Kleenex. On the count of three everyone has to look at a dirty picture and start wanking. The first fellow to go off is the winner. And to make it more fun, the last one gets his head flushed in the lavatory. In case you don't have a dirty book, I've provided a suitable picture here. Good, isn't it?

Word Puzzle

Instead of English homework, why not try this literary teaser tonight. My favourite swear word is hidden in this little word grid. Can you spot it?

B	J	E	F	R	C	V	E
B	O	L	L	O	C	K	S
W	O	N	O	T	T	I	C
J	U	V	T	B	L	F	C
O	P	Q	A	A	B	V	K

Botty Wiping

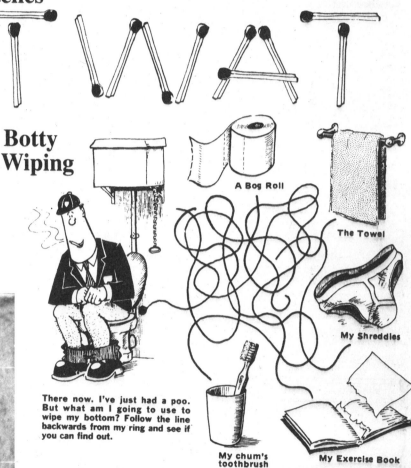

A Bog Roll

The Towel

My Shreddies

My chum's toothbrush

My Exercise Book

There now. I've just had a poo. But what am I going to use to wipe my bottom? Follow the line backwards from my ring and see if you can find out.

Graffiti Game

Look what I've drawn on the top of my desk while teacher wasn't looking! But on the second picture I've made a few changes. How many can you spot?

ANSWERS

Let's see how you did! **Swearing with Matches:** The only one I can manage is 'SHIT', with a big 'H'. I hope you got a few more. **Botty Wiping:** It was my best chum's toothbrush, of course. **Graffiti Game:** I've put some spunk coming out the end. And drawn some this next to it.

INSIDE THE
TORCH

Fumble about in any young schoolboy's pocket and you're bound to put your hand on something long and hard. His torch. He uses it to find marbles under chairs, to find the outside lavatory at night, and to read his father's photographic magazines under the bedclothes. We all take the torch for granted, but what do we really know about the mysterious workings of this scientific wonder?

KEY to TORCH

(1) The Handle.
(2) The Battery.
(3) Another Battery.
(4) Torch Hook.
(5) The Bulb.
(6) Another Battery.
(7) The Front of the Torch.

HOW THE TORCH WORKS

The power for the torch is kept inside the batteries (2, 3 and 6). These are housed in the handle (1). The torch is operated using the Switch (not shown) and the power, or 'electricity', travels up the batteries (2, 3 and 6) in volts, or 'amps' and enters the bulb (5). Light then comes out the end of the torch (7).

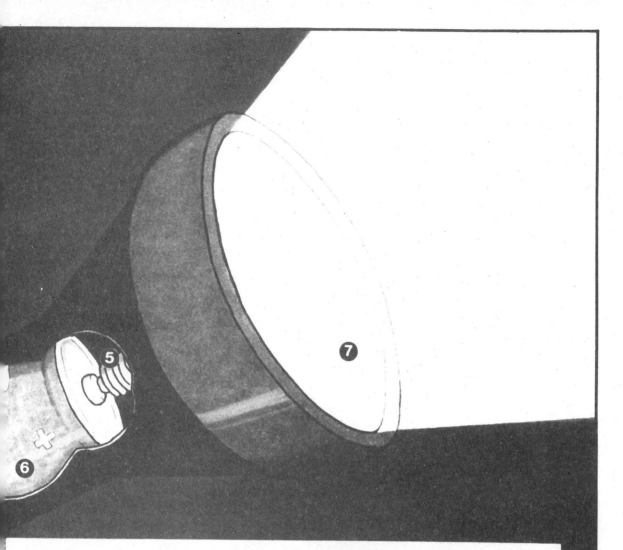

TORCHES IN ACTION

Torches are used every day by different people to do different things.   Here are just two uses for the torch.

A zoo keeper using a torch to find a monkey.

A cowboy using a torch to find a Red Indian.

Letters to the Editor

SpunkRag 2008

Grant Wankshaft - Rag Editor

WELL guys and gals, rag week is upon us once more! *(that's the Spunkbridge University Rag Week, not the one that girls have once a month!!!)* SpunkRag is the week when *(I didn't mean that last thing in a sexist way, by the way. Obviously. Female physiology is nothing to make cheap jokes about. It happens to be very beautiful, actually. No, really.)* SpunkRag is the week when *(I wasn't trying to be patronising to girls or anything there, talking about their physiology being beautiful. I mean men's physiology is very beautiful, too, don't get me wrong. Not that I'm a puff, you understand. Obviously.)* SpunkRag is the week *(not that there's anything wrong with being queer... I mean GAY. Some of my best friends are gay, actually and I treat them as if they are*

completely normal.) SpunkRag is the week when us students all go utterly bonkers and do mental things to help ordinary people much less fortunate than ourselves. And you've been writing to the drunken, wacky Rag Comittee telling us about your efforts to raise cash for local poor people. **Pity we were all too drunk to read your letters!!!!!!!!!!!!!!** *(That was a joke. Alcohol addiction is a serious problem, actually).* Here's a selection of your wackiest money-raising stunts...

Pail Imitation

☐ SpunkRag claim that every penny raised goes towards funding worthy causes at home and abroad. That's not true, because last rag week I collected £250 going round the campus with a bucket and I kept the fucking lot.

A Bell
Chemistry Dept.

☐ Last rag week, I emptied two hundred tins of baked beans into my bath and sat in it for nearly three days. It was a huge success, and thanks to the generosity of my sponsors I raised £18.56, enough to buy 60 tins of beans for a village in Africa or somewhere like that.

S Peters
Rolf Harris Hall

☐ Like the previous correspondent, I also had the stunningly original idea of sitting in a bath of baked beans. Unfortunately, after sitting in it for a week, I realised that I had forgotten to get sponsored, or even inform anyone that I was doing it. I felt a right twat.

R Fellows
Bagpuss Hall

☐ After sitting in a bath of baked beans for a week as a zany rag stunt, I was shocked to discover that the beans had set hard and I was unable to get out. I would like to thank te Spunkbridge Fire Brigade who promptly came to my aid, and scraped me into a pedal bin with an enormous fork.

R Townshend
Austin Powers Hall

☐ My girlfriend told me she was going to sit in a bath of beans to raise money for SpunkRag. Imagine my dismay when I went upstairs and found her in the tub with Rowan Atkinson and him out of 'Sharpe'.

C. Head
Zoology Dept.

☐ Rag week is supposed to be about having fun, but when I tried to sit in a tin of beans I only succeeded in cutting my arse wide open on the jagged rim. Where's the fun in that?

M. Radcliffe
American Studies Dept.

Medical Records

I am a medical student, and me and my mates have just pushed someone on a wheeled hospital bed, covering a distance of nearly 350 miles. We weren't doing it for charity, it's just that some old woman came into casualty with a broken hip and we were looking for a ward that could take her.

R. Binnersley
Spunkbridge Med. School

I'm a third-year English Literature student and this SpunkRag me and my fellow course members will be raising money not by sitting in beans, but by attending a marathon reading of the complete works of Shakespeare. We intend to spot and laugh mirthlessly at all 18 jokes to show how clever we are, and we'd like people to pledge money for every joke we spot and laugh at. The event starts at 6.00am at the Arts Centre, and the laughing will be opened at 11.30 by Germaine Greer who will guffaw at the line "A plague, o' these pickle Herring!" (Two Gentlemen of Verona, Act 2, Scene 3).

Lucy Ringpiece
Spongebob Squarepants Hall

Charity begins at home, or so they say. So how come I stood with a SpunkRag collection tin in my front room all day last Saturday and raised fuck all?

V. Soskin
Nookie Bear Hall

This rag week, I will be cooking a variety of dishes and charging people to eat them. However, I will be keeping all the proceeds as I am not a student, but a restaurateur open for business, and I don't believe in all this charity nonsense.

A. Bacon
Cambridge

Ballet good show

During college rag week, my friend thought it might be a laugh to go to college dressed in a frilly tutu and tights. However, nobody turned a hair as she is a student at the Royal School of Ballet.

D McGurk
Fox Mulder Hall

It's amazing how many people miss the point of rag week completely. This year, for instance, my friend intends to sit for twenty four hours in a bath of spaghetti hoops.

J. Hedgecock
Peace Studies

On March 12th, I intend to sit in a bath of warm soapy water for twenty minutes, and wonder if anyone would like to sponsor me in this wacky stunt?

S. Dawes
East Mosely

Atomic Relief

The current record for purity of Helium stands at 2 parts in 10^{15}, ie 2 in a million billion. I am a third year physics student, and this rag week I intend to raise money by breaking this record and obtain the isotope Helium 4 (^{4}He) with impurity levels of only 1 part in 10^{15}... whilst sitting in a bath of baked beans.

A. Haxby
Swindon

I'm all for charity, me, but I certainly won't be filling my bath with baked beans during Spunkbridge University rag Week. That's because I'm the Mayor of Bath, and it would cost far too much

in beans, to mention nothing of the clean-up operation afterwards.

Ray Cliffe,
Mayor of Bath

I'm in the Spunkbridge University Second XV Rugby squad and last night we held a sponsored 'Behaving in a Seemly Fashion Marathon' in the Union Bar. For 24 hours we intended to wear men's clothes, avoid setting fire to our farts, refrain from incoherent singing of indecorous songs, and keep our cocks out of each other's beer. However, we didn't raise much money because after 9 minutes our prop forward put on a pair of women's stockings and shat into a pint pot.

Luke Bore
Chemical Engineering

I intend to spend this rag week sitting in a bath of baked beans... *whilst sitting in a bath of baked beans.* Would anyone like to sponsor me?

P. Ferris
Archaeology

TOP TIPS

WHEN filling a bath with beans, open all the tins at the bottom. Sedimented beans then come out without the need for excessive shaking.

S. Greene
Botany Dept.

STUDENTS. Unfunny fund-raising events can instantly be made hilarious by wearing women's clothes. Except if you are a woman.

T Hooper
Engineering Dept.

A TIN of baked beans cut in half lengthwise make an ideal pair of baths of baked beans for a couple of zany hamsters to sit in for charity.

S. Thornton
Chumbawumba Hall

A COUPLE of thimbles and some pipe-cleaners will make an ideal ladies' bra for a male, rugby-playing hamster to wear whilst sitting in a bath of baked beans.

T. Cairns
Theatre Choreography Yr3

35

SID the SEXIST

featuring *BAZ, BOB* and *JOE*

in a feature length farrago of filth

For Whom The Bells Toll

...SORRY I'M LATE, SIDNEY, ONLY THE PRAYER MEETING WENT ON A BIT. ANYWAY, I'M LOOKING FORWARD TO THE NIGHTCLUB...

...ONLY SOFT DRINKS FOR YOU, THOUGH SIDNEY... YOU'VE GOT TO BE UP EARLY TOMORROW. WE'RE GOING TO CHOOSE THE ENGAGEMENT RINGS, REMEMBER?

SHORTLY... ...BLAH! BLAH! BLAH!...SO YOUR SIDE IS HAVING YELLOW CARNATIONS AND MY SIDE WHITE LILLIES, WHAT DO *YOU* THINK? AND REMIND ME TO ORDER THE CORSAGE AND CAN YOU CUT A FEW GUESTS FROM YOUR SIDE, ONLY THERE'S FAR TOO MANY...

INSIDE... ......BUT I JUST CAN'T DECIDE BETWEEN IVORY WITH THE SCALLOPED EDGE AND OLD ENGLISH SCRIPT OR THE PLAIN OFF-WHITE WITH THE CRINKLED EDGE AND THE SILVER SERIF TYPE, MUMMY LIKES IVORY BUT I'M NOT SURE AND WHAT ABOUT THE CAKE, MUMMY SAYS WE MUST HAVE PILLARS ON THE CAKE, IT'S NOT A PROPER WEDDING UNLESS THERE'S PILLARS ON THE CAKE, SO MUMMY SAYS HOW MANY PILLARS DO YOU WANT, SIDNEY, HOW MANY PILLARS DO YOU WANT, SIDNEY? PILLARS PILLARS HOW MANY PILLARS, SIDNEY, PILLARS SIDNEY, PILLARS, HOW MANY...?

ERM... ERM...

...WELL YOU THINK ABOUT IT. I'M OFF TO THE LITTLE LADIES ROOM TO POWDER MY NOSE.

WAIT HERE FOR ME.

HI, THERE...

...I'VE BEEN WATCHING YOU. YOU'RE MY KIND OF GUY. FANCY COMING BACK TO MY PLACE FOR A NIGHT OF THE WILDEST SEX YOU'VE EVER HAD?

GUMPH!

OH, DEAR! LOOKS LIKE I'M TOO LATE. I FANCIED GETTING *MY* DIRTY HANDS ON HIM.

NOT TO WORRY. YOU COME BACK TO MY PLACE AS WELL... I THINK THERE'S ENOUGH OF HIM TO GO ROUND... AND I'VE GOT A *VERY BIG BED*.

44

NEXT EVENING...

SUR, BAZ... TELL US AGAIN, WHY AM I DRESSED AS A LASS?

AALREET JOE, HERE WE GAN...

...IN TWO MINUTES TIME, SID'S WENDY IS GUNNA WAALK THROUGH THE DOOR FO' TU MEET SID. WHEN SHE DOES, SHE'S GUNNA CATCH 'IM SNOGGIN' WI' ANOTHER LASS... ...YEE!

SHE TEKS A JEALOUS RADGE AN' CAALLS THE WEDDIN' OFF... SID'S PROBLEMS SOLVED.

BUT WHY COULDN'T WIZ GET A PROPER LASS?

I'VE TELT YUZ. WU COULDN'T FIND ONE WHAT WAS PREPARED TU SNOG SID, LIKE.

ME SISTER WOULD'VE DONE IT.

YOUR SISTER LOOKS LESS LIKE A FUCKIN' LASS THAN YEE DEE, JOE MAN.

I'LL SECOND THAT. SHE'S A FUCKIN' PIG, JOE.

WELL, I STILL DIVVEN'T SEE WHY IT HAD T'BE ME WHAT DRESSED UP!

WELL, IT'S SIMPLY 'COZ YOU'RE THE FUCKIN' THICKEST OOT THE LOT O'WUZ.

AYE, I SUPPURZ.

ANYWAYS, JUST REMEMBER: SNOG SID WHEN SHE COMES IN...

YU DID TELL 'ER EIGHT O'CLOCK, DIDN'T YU, SID?

AYE. EIGHT O'CLOCK.

OKAY JOE! HERE SHE IS.

SNOG! SNOG! SLURP!

MMMMPH!

?

46

47

NEXT DAY...

HOW! WHERE'S ME TWENTY POOND, WOR BOB?

THERE YU GAN. NOW PUT YER ARM ROOND SID AN' WAALK PAST TAAT HAMMA SHOP.

PUT ME ARM ROOND 'IM? Y'NEVER SAID OWT ABOOT *THAT*. IT'S AN EXTRA TENNER T'PUT ME ARM ROOND 'IM.

FUCKIN' HELL. IT'S A MAN'S LIFE AT STAKE HERE, BOBETTE, WOMAN... JESUS!... I'LL GIVE IT T'YU WHEN WE GET BACK YEM.

SO...

EH?! THAT'S *SIDNEY!*

"KING SLEDGE" SALE ITEM

CLAW & BALL

PIN & LUMP

OY!! SIDNEY!

48

FRIDAY AFTERNOON...

THE FOX AND HOOND

PUBLIC BAR

FUCK ME, LADS... I'M FINISHED.

THIS TIME THE MORRO' I'LL BE MR. WENDY FUCKIN' HAYSTACKS... NEXT STOP THE PRAM SHOP. THEN IT'S DOONHILL TU THE CREMATORIUM VIA THE FUCKIN' GARDEN CENTRE.

CHEER UP, MAN. WUZ'VE STILL GOT YER STAG NEET TU GAN. WE'LL SEND YEE OOT WI' A BANG AT THE UNION CLUB.

AYE. WE'RE GANNIN' TU SEE THAT COMEDIAN BLURK, CHUBBY ARSE...

... AN' EIGHT STRIPPAZ FROM NOTTINGHAM.

AYE... I SEEN THEM AT SOOTH SHIELDS. CLASS ACT, SID. FIRE BANANAS OOT THEIR TWATS THE' DEE.

AYE. THEN THEY SHAG AALL THE AUDIENCE ON STAGE IN THE SECOND HALF.

ME AN' ME DAD WENT UP LAST TIME.

SUR C'MON, SID MAN, SUP UP, GAN YEM AN' PUT SOME CLEAN UNDAKEX ON. WUZ'LL SEE YU THERE AT SIX.

6.00 PM...

UNION CLUB

NUFC

TONITE CHUBBY ARSE + STRIPPERS

HERE HE COMES, LADS. THE CONDEMNED MAN, ABOOT TU SHAG A HEARTY STRIPPER!

PARSNIPS ENGINEERING

AALL REET, LADS? STAG DO, IS IT?

AYE... THIS UN.

POOR CUNT.

... LISTEN, SIT HIM AT THE FRONT, THEN WHEN THE SHAGGIN' STARTS HE'LL BE FOG UP.

REET. THANKS, PAL.

YANK!

NEXT DAY...

54

10
THINGS YOU *NEVER KNEW* ABOUT
FUND-RAISING

WHETHER they're standing plastic figures with slots in their heads outside newsagents, or selling dead people's Mantovani records in shops smelling of mothballs, charities need to raise funds. And no-one gives more to charity than the British. It seems every supermarket fag counter is clogged with big hearted Brits spending more than they can afford on lottery tickets in a desperate attempt to give money to worthy causes. But how much do you actually know about fund-raising? Here's 10 fact packed charitable contributions.

A red-faced Princip is led away by Yugoslav police.

1 The first ever fund-raising event was in the Stone Age when five cave men dressed in Stone Age women's underwear and pushed a granite bed around the town to raise money to build a henge. Sponsorship forms were printed on stone tablets, but it proved impossible to collect any of the cash, as money was not invented until 2 million years later in 630 BC.

2 The smallest man ever to raise money was the fairytale character Tom Thumb, 2 inches tall, who tap-danced on the bottom of a cup for 28 weeks, stopping only to drink water out of a thimble. Ironically, this feat broke the record for the smallest sum raised for charity at only 8 pence.

3 Conversely, the largest sum raised in a sponsored event was £31 billion, raised during a five mile sponsored walk by Bolton schoolboy Mark Crowther. He managed this feat by asking his father to take his sponsor form to work, where everyone pledged a penny per mile. His father worked at China.

4 Unlucky student Giles Millington set out in 1976 on a sponsored jail-break, dressed as a convict. He had covered 108 miles when he was picked up by 2 over-zealous members of the West Mercia Constabulary and taken to the cells. Following a series of bizarre administrative errors, he was give a 40-year jail sentence without parole which he is currently serving in Wakefield High Security Prison. He raised £52.60, but has been unable to collect it.

5 Spaceman Neil Armstrong was promised $240 for a donkey sanctuary if he sat in a bath of baked beans on the moon. NASA officials agreed and packed his 'Eagle' lunar module with a cast iron bath and 400 tins of beans. However, on landing on the Sea of Tranquillity in July 1969, he realised he had left the tin opener in a drawer at Mission Control.

6 American scientists researching fund-raising have discovered that ginger-haired people on average give 17% more to charity than proper people. Consequently, fund raising events do less well in the Summer months when ginger people are forced indoors to avoid being burned to a crisp.

7 The Crusades, a sort of Comic Relief in reverse where happy people abroad were made to suffer, was the biggest fund raising event ever. Eight shillings and sixpence (equivalent to £10,000,000,000 nowadays) was raised by a tithe on all tenanted land and chattels, a poll tax on the peasantry and a bring-and-buy sale in the front garden at Westminster Abbey.

8 The Biggest blunder during a fund-raising event occured in the 1914 Rag Week at the University of Sarajevo. Student Gavrilo Princip, a hit squad member, took what he thought was a can of Silly String out of his pocket in order to spray Archduke Franz Ferdinand in the face. It turned out to be a revolver, and he inadvertently precipitated a war that was to kill or injure almost 45 million people.

9 Fund-raising in the year 2020 will be very different from what it is now. Instead of notes and coins, sponsors will pledge computerised 'credits' down a wire to a bank hundreds of miles away using a magnetic strip on a thin piece of plastic, no bigger than a credit card.

10 Not only that, but baked beans and custard pies will be redundant. Students will sit in a bath containing a small pill, and hit squads will gunge victims using digital custard sent via the internet.

Armstrong looking for a tin-opener.

16,000 Fathoms to DEATH!

August 1943. Regular convoys plough across the perilous waters of the North Atlantic, providing a vital lifeline between America and the beleagured allied forces. The heavy laden vessels make easy pickings for the dreaded underwater nazi menace – the 'U' boats.

HMS Osprey is one of several Mercury Destroyer-class frigate carriers charged with the unenviable task of escorting the convoys on their treacherous journey.

On the bridge, Captain 'Spikey' Beaumont DSO anxiously scours the horizon for the danger which may strike at any moment...

IT'S QUIET, MALTRAVERS... TOO QUIET. I DON'T LIKE IT.

CHIN UP, SKIP. TWO MORE DAYS IN THIS TUB AND WE'RE BACK IN BLIGHTY.

DAMN THIS TIN LEG!

Beaumont, veteran of over a dozen sea battles, lost his leg whilst erecting flat pack self-assembly shelving in the living room of his home in Bakewell, Derbyshire.

AHOY, CAPTAIN. MOVEMENT OFF THE PORT BOW. LOOKS LIKE WE'VE GOT COMPANY.

LET'S SEE.

IT COULD BE NOTHING, BUT I'D BETTER TAKE UP A LANCASTER FOR A CLOSER LOOK.

DAMN THIS ARM!

Beaumont fights a losing battle to keep control of the airborne giant. Spikey, veteran of many dogfights and with over 100 kills to his credit, lost his left arm below the elbow whilst putting up a larchwood lattice trellis at his mother's bungalow in Pinner.

Seconds later, Spikey Beaumont is wrestling with the controls of one of Osprey's eight Avro Lancaster reconnaissance heavy artillery bombers.

SPIKEY'S IN THE BRINEY. HE'S PRANGED HIS KITE.

BAD SHOW, SKIPPER.

BETTER LUCK NEXT TIME EH, OLD CHAP.

Meanwhile, an unseen enemy lurks nearby...

ACHTUNG! ES IST EIN SITTING DUCK. PREPARE ZE TORPEDOS - UNT BE SCHNELL ABOUT IT.

JAWOHL MEIN KAPITAN.

Captain Fritz Obergruppenfuhrer ran a tight ship aboard U-113, pride of the Luftwaffe's dreaded submarine fleet.

Back on board Osprey...

DID YOU RECCY JERRY WHILST YOU WERE UP, SPIKEY OLD BOY?

NEVER SAW A BALLY THING, GINGER. DAMN THESE GLASS EYES!

An Olympic gold medal winning marksman, Spikey Beaumont had tragically lost both his eyes whilst pinning up bunting at his Auntie Jean's local church fete in Wimbourne

I SAY - IT'S VERA LYNNS BIRTHDAY. ANYONE FOR BUBBLY?

OH I SAY. GOOD SHOW.

TOP HOLE.

WELL, CHIN CHIN.

DOWN THE HATCH, WHAT.

Suddenly...

SORRY TO SPOIL THE PARTY, CHAPS, BUT WE'VE TAKEN A DIRECT HIT. PORT BOW.

THE OLD GIRL'S TAKING ON WATER AND ALL THAT. IT'S NOT LOOKING TOO CHIPPER. DAMN NUISANCE.

HA HA. ICH BIN EIN DIRECT HIT.

ABANDON SHIP!

U113

Spikey, Lieutenant 'Ginger' Trubshaw, and 1st engineer 'Chalky' Scott scrambled into Osprey's lifeboat...

I'M A BIT PECKISH. ANYONE BRING THE HAMPER?

YES, ME SKIP.

RIGHT. WHO'S FOR BATTENBURG CAKE?

I SAY, ANY SIGN OF JERRY YET?

NOT YET, OLD BEAN. BUT HE'LL BE BACK TO FINISH US OFF...

...AND WE'LL BE SITTING DUCKS.

WAIT A MOMENT. WHAT'S THIS?

I THOUGHT SO. IT'S ONE OF OSPREY'S TORPEDO TUBES AND A BOX OF DYNAMITE.

OH, WIZARD SKIPPER.

LET'S FACE IT CHAPS, WE'RE IN A BIT OF A PICKLE. BUT I'VE GOT A PLAN AND IT JUST MIGHT WORK.

GOOD SHOW, SPIKEY. LET'S GIVE IT A WHIRL.

The fearless skiper packed his mouth and hat with dynamite before loading himself into the salvaged torpedo tube.

BREAK A LEG, SKIP.

5...4...3...2...1...

...FIRE!

NOW TO TEACH THAT SQUAREHEAD A LESSON HE WON'T FORGET IN A HURRY.

TALLY HO! SPIKEY'S BANG ON COURSE!

AAARGH!

The stricken U-boat sank in seconds.

HOORAH!

Moments later...

WELL DONE, SKIPPER. BULLSEYE!

THANKS CHAPS. BUT BOY, HAVE I GOT A SORE HEAD!

Between October 1943 and August 1947, 436 German submarines were destroyed by the English navy in the North Atlantic. Thanks to the bravery of men like 'Spikey' Beaumont, vital convoys were able to reach their destinations, and allied forces gained control of the seas. Britannia once again ruled the waves, Hitler was routed in Europe and peace returned to the World. Beaumont finished the war as a rear Admiral in the RAF, and was killed in 1949 whilst repairing a bird table in the garden of his cousin Nora's house just outside Barrow-in-Furness. He was posthumously awarded the Victoria Cross by a grateful nation.

THE END

ANIMALS at WAR

Ask any schoolboy who always wins the war and he'll tell you – Britain! That's because when it comes to winning wars the British are jolly well best. But it's not just our soldiers' spunk that sees off Johnny Foreigner time and time again. Over the years the British army has relied heavily on help from the animal kingdom. And its not just our four legged friend the horse who has served King and Country.

An army marches on its stomach, and during World War Two British generals considered many ways of poisoning the German food supplies. One short lived experiment was to parachute British cows, injected with deadly poison, into the fields of France.

However, the operation was a failure. Of 750 poisonous cows dropped behind enemy lines only two successfully deployed their parachutes. One suffered four broken ankles and was eaten by the French resistance, resulting in four cases of mild diarrhoea, while the other landed in a tree where it eventually starved to death.

However, all was not lost. One of the other 748 cattle which plummeted to their deaths landed on a small German motor pool in the town of Alsace, causing £45 worth of damage to a motorcycle side-car combination.

After several unsuccessful attempts by the R.A.F. to destroy the strategically vital Van de Haber railway bridge at Den Haag in Holland, the S.A.S. devised an incredible plan to sabotage the timber-built structure by introducing woodworm to its supporting piers.

Under cover of darkness, three crack S.A.S. frogmen swam 100 miles up the river Amstal before boring holes in the timbers of the bridge and releasing six specially trained woodworm larvae. Unfortunately, the daring plan was foiled when, early the following morning, a keen-eyed German guard spotted the telltale holes in the structure and called in Hitler's crack timber treatment division, the K.G.S. (Kuprinohl Gussellte Schtad), who successfully treated the affected timbers.

Ironically, the bridge collapsed shortly after the war due to an undetected outbreak of dry rot in the unexposed base of one of the piers.

Nowadays, squirrels are often looked upon as a pest. But in Britain's hour of need, even they had a key role to play. Professor Thomas Woodhead, a War Ministry research scientist at the top secret Bletchley Park research establishment, trained a dozen grey squirrels to relentlessly follow about and annoy several top ranking German officials. 'Woodhead's Squirrels' were a remarkable success, and became a vital weapon in the Allied arsenal. They successfully pestered and upset many top ranking Nazi targets, causing many of them to become extremely agitated and eventually lose their tempers. Their most famous victim was Hitler's deputy Rudolf Hess. After being pestered by a squirrel for nearly two years, he eventually cracked, and flew to Britain to surrender, a broken man.

Lieutenant Colonel 'Spikey' Tolhurst became better known as the 'Butterfly man of Colditz' after his dramatic escape from the notorious Nazi P.O.W. camp. Unknown to his German captors, Tolhurst, whose real legs had both been confiscated following persistent escape attempts, kept a secret stash of over 500 caterpillars in the hollow metal replacements which he had been given.

After the butterflies had hatched, Tolhurst strapped them onto his body using strands of his own hair. He then clapped his hands loudly and the startled butterflies immediately took off, hauling him to freedom over the top of the 80-foot electronic fence and past astounded Nazi guards. Once over the fence, Tolhurst caught a bus to England, where, after the war, he opened Britain's first butterfly hospital, which went bankrupt in 1947.

So many British bomber crews were lost over Germany during the war the Government ordered the R.A.F. to train monkeys to fly bombing missions. However, only one bombing mission was ever flown manned by monkeys. On a cold November morning in 1943 a Lancaster bomber, manned by six monkeys and a marmoset, took off from R.A.F. Milfield, in Northumberland, with a deadly cargo bound for Germany's industrial heartland, the Ruhr Valley.

However, four hours later the plane had to be destroyed by R.A.F. Spitfires after it had unloaded its entire cargo of bombs on the Welsh holiday town of Rhyl, killing 64 civilians. A cover-up was launched, and the incident officially blamed on a stray Nazi bomber. The monkey experiment was abandoned, and all records of it destroyed.

The Allies made several unsuccessful attempts to assassinate Hitler during the war. Perhaps the most unsuccessful of all was that codenamed 'Operation Jaws'. The plan was for a deadly man-eating Great White Shark to attack and kill the Fuhrer in front of a million of his supporters at a rally in Nuremburg. A suitable shark was captured by the Australian navy off the coast of Queensland, and transported in a large watertight box to an airfield in Scotland. The 30-foot fish was then suspended by its tail from a Spitfire at the end of a 100-foot rope, and flown to its target by a volunteer pilot. As the Fuhrer addressed the crowds the pilot made an inch-perfect swooping pass, and the vicious shark's jaws passed within snapping distance of Hitler's moustache. Unfortunately the fish had died during the 500-mile flight across the Channel, and Hitler, who appeared shocked and confused, escaped with his life.

The British were not the only ones to recruit animals during the war. Towards the end of 1944, with Monty's Eighth Army swiftly advancing across North Africa, German Field Marshall Rommel found himself desperately short of armourments. In a last gasp effort to thwart the British advance he ordered 200 elephants to be painted like tanks to fool Montgomery into over-estimating the strength of the German forces.

However, the elephants made less than convincing tanks, and after walking up and down for a couple of days they became restless and wandered off back to the jungle in search of food and water. Within weeks the Nazi hold on Africa had been broken.

SHAG FOR VICTORY

FAT SLAGS
COMMANDO ACTION LIBRARY

Nº346

AIEEEEEE!

AUGUST 1942 – AND IN THE SKIES ABOVE FULCHESTER A DESPERATE BATTLE IS BEING FOUGHT. IT IS A FIGHT TO THE DEATH BETWEEN THE BRAVE FLY-BOYS OF ENGLAND'S CRACK RAF FIGHTER SQUADRONS AND THE EVIL SAUSAGE-EATING SQUAREHEADS OF HITLER'S LÜFTWAFFE.

LATER...

EEH. MY BACK'S FUCKIN' KILLIN' ME.

AYE. BUT IT'S NICE T'KNOW YER DOIN' YER BIT FER THE WAR EFFORT.

DOIN' OWT TONIGHT, SAN?

NOT MUCH. THEZ AN EYE-TIE P.O.W. ON THE NEXT FARM. I PROMISED 'IM I'D SUCK 'IM OFF BEHIND THE PIG STY

I WOULDN'T BOTHER. 'E FUCKED ME AT DINNERTIME WHEN YOU WENT FER A SHIT.

HE WERE CRAP. I THINK THEY MUST'VE GORRIMON SHORT RATIONS OR SUMMAT.

I KNOW. LET'S GO T'THE MUNITIONS FACTORY.

WHAT FOH?

GLEN MILLER'S DOIN' A CONCERT IN THE CANTEEN. THEZ BOUND T'BE LOADS O'YANKS THERE!

'OW WE GUNNUGET THERE? THEZ NO BUSES OR OWT.

P. GUTHRIE G SONS
MUNITIONS FACTORY

BBC OUTSIDE BROADCAST UNIT

THE HARDEST VIDEOS WE'VE EVER SOLD - BUT THAT'S NOT SAYING VERY MUCH

All these videos are absolutely un-cut as there is absolutely nothing in them remotely explicit enough to warrant censorship of any kind.

YOU WON'T HAVE SEEN ANYTHING LIKE IT IN ADULT VIDEOS BEFORE!

£27.95 ea.
or 4 for £100

SEXTH FORM PREFECTS

What happens when two sexually frustrated blonde sixth form nymphettes find themselves alone in the dormitory on a hot summer's night with just a selection of sex toys to keep them company? We don't know, and you won't find out from this video starring a couple of bored looking 48 year-old slappers in wigs. Half-heartedly dressed as sixth form schoolgirls, they quickly get down to business on a bunk bed in the back of a warehouse in Peckham, disinterestedly rubbing each others' tits for eight minutes to a soundtrack of mains humming. And that's it. **Price £27.95.**

HOT, HARD 'N' HORNY

Big John is a plumber who is called out by a horny 36DD housewife to change the washer on her tap. When that job is done, she gives him another - a blow job! And she finds out he's got a 10 inch tool in his overalls. You really have to see it to believe it. However, you **don't** see it, just six minutes of the back of her head moving up and down intercut with close-ups of him screwing his face up. We guarantee you will be **shocked** by how much you have paid for this truly shit film. **Price £27.95.**

HOT, HARD 'n' HORNY

BUY NOW BEFORE WE'RE PROSECUTED UNDER THE TRADES DESCRIPTION ACT

WARNING!
These videos are very unfulfilling, and we urge anyone who is easily disappointed not to buy them. They depict tame **SEXUAL ACTS**, in some cases of a blurred or wobbly nature that many viewers may find risible. It is not our intention to **AROUSE** or **EXCITE** the viewer, merely to mislead them into **PARTING** with their **HARD** earned cash without **BREAKING THE LAW** and indeed embarrass them into not asking for their **MONEY BACK.**

WIDE OPEN AND WILLING

Cindy Smallpiece, a 38DD sex mad red-head just loves to dress up. She finds putting on her black fishnet stockings, split crotch panties and black stilettoes a real turn-on... but not as big a turn-on as taking them off! However, despite featuring heavily on the packaging, she's not actually in the video, which features a stripper with flu from Stoke Newington hurriedly taking her clothes off in the back of a warehouse in Clapham in return for fifty quid cash. With wow and flutter soundtrack of cheesy music from a battery operated cassette recorder, this will be one of the least erotic experiences of your life. **Price £27.95.**

8 WAY SEX PLAY

EIGHT WAY SEX PLAY

When four well hung studs meet four big titted chicks, the permutations are incalculable. It's everyone's ultimate fantasy, as the guys and girls do it in every possible (and some impossible!) position including sandwich, 'A' and 'O'. This is the hardest film we've ever seen, but due to heavy re-editing for legal reasons, it's unlikely to be the hardest **you've** ever seen. Shot in the seventies on super 8 and recently transferred to video by projecting it onto a warehouse door, the whole sorry four minutes is accompanied by the sound of the projector turning over and somebody reversing a van outside. Just as something vaguely sexy starts to happen, the film sticks and melts before your very eyes. Deeply dreadful. **Price £27.95.**

FREE!!

With every order we receive, we'll send you, absolutely FREE a quality love doll. Always willing and always available, these sex dolls will fulfill your every need, providing you're turned on by orange paddling pool vinyl and that you're not too dizzy after twenty minutes blowing it up. Well stacked with tits that look and feel like the half footballs that they are and equipped with 3 (yes 3!) inviting orrifices, each with a razor sharp welded plastic seam guaranteed to cut your old man to ribbons in the unlikely event that you get aroused enough to try and shag it.
Buy ALL 4 videos, and receive the deluxe model with vaginal vibral unit plus vibrating throb control mouth, which will do nothing for you but will certainly affect next door's television reception, leaving them in no doubt as to what you're up to. Requires 24 AA batteries (not supplied).

Yes! I want you to have my home address and credit card details. Please send me the following videos.

☐ SEXTH FORM PREFECTS
☐ HOT HARD 'N' HORNY
☐ WIDE OPEN AND WILLING
☐ EIGHT WAY SEX PLAY

Send to: Randy Bollocks Porn Products, PO Box 1, Peckham.

Name................ ...Address.......................... Credit Card No. ....

If I'm not completely satisfied, and I won't be I can return the videos for you to sell to some other poor sod with full nuts. I will recieve a cheque for the full amount drawn on the account of *Randy Bollocks Porn Products* with pictures of dildos drawn on it and the words ' Porn Video Refund' written on in big letters, which I will not dare take into my bank. I accept that this is my own fault.

71

THE INSULT THAT MADE A SEXIST OUT OF "CEDRIC"

Let Me PROVE I Can Make YOU a SEXIST!

ARE you "fed up" with overweight, beer swilling animals getting all the laughs in the pub by lighting farts and doing "last turkey in the shop"? Sick and tired of having to go to the toilet for a wee after a puny six or seven pints, when we all know that the top shelf tarts won't drop 'em for any man who can't swallow at least a gallon before straining his potatoes? I know just how you feel because, believe it or not, I used to be HALF A MAN too!

My Secret

Then I discovered a wonderful way to develop sexism fast. It worked wonders for me - changed me from a polite ten stone nobody who never got a sniff of kipper to a sweaty fourteen stone brass-necked gob-shite who has to beat back the high end skirt (who swallow) with a shitty stick.

My patented five point plan involves 300 minutes a day of pleasant practice in the privacy of your room or shed. My method involves no weights, pulleys or springs, just simple things you already have in the home: 120 Embassy Regal, 36 large cans of lager, a boil-in-the-bag curry and the Freemans catalogue. This method has already helped thousands of other fellows become bloated mindless wankers like me in double quick time.

I will make you a Sexist FAST

If you're like I was, you'll want a galvanised kebab proof digestive system and mindlessly offensive personality you can be proud of anytime. You'll want the Jocky Wilson type physique and flatulent personal magnetism that women rave about at the beach or pub. The kind that makes other fellows green with envy.

Sidney Smutt

Awarded the title "The World's Most Sexist Man"

The Adventures of FELIX CRUSOE and his AMAZING UNDERPANTS!

As originally featured in *Viz Tuppenny Illustrated Paper For Boys Own Penny Comic Illustrated, 1887. Written by Brigadier Rudyard Lewerthwaite of His Majesty's Royal Mounted Stamps, VSO, JCB, DFC and Bar. Plum. Nudge.*

The date is 1865 and the HMS Dalmation is bound for the uncharted coast of South America in search of exotic fruits and vegetables to be made into soaps, anti dandruff shampoos and shower gels for the Crown heads of Europe.

Felix's log; Underpant date: 5th May, 1865. We have been 8 months at sea, and still no sign of land. My underpants are holding up well, but unless we reach port soon, the elastic may begin to fray...

I THINK I'LL CLIMB INTO MY HAMMOCK FOR A SHORT REST.

READER'S VOICE

BUT FELIX... YOU HAVEN'T GOT A HAMMOCK!

THAT'S WHERE YOU'RE WRONG! BY STRETCHING MY MIRACULOUS UNDERPANTS 'TWIXT TWO CABIN HOOKS MY KEX FASHION A SPLENDID HAMMOCK.

ZZZZZZ!

Now with pants a'plenty Felix set about building himself a Shreddies shelter...

THIS WILL BE MY UNDERPANT HOME UNTIL I AM RESCUED.

And he put his pants to good use hunting and gathering food.

HA! GOTCHA! MY OUTSTRETCHED 'Y' FRONTS MAKE A NIFTY FISHING NET!

AND USING THESE TROLLEYS AS A SLING...

WHOOSH!

..I CAN CATCH COCONUTS!

I WILL ALSO NEED CLOTHES TO PROTECT ME FROM THE ELEMENTS...

THERE, PANT-PERFECT!

One morning while Felix was patrolling the shore...

WHAT'S THAT ON THE HORIZON? IT CAN'T BE! I DON'T BELIEVE IT!

SHIP AHOY! I'M SAVED AT LAST!

Hastily rubbing his nylon pants to create a spark, Felix ignited a huge underpant beacon to attract the ship's attention.

OH NO! THEY CAN'T HAVE SEEN ME! THEY'RE SAILING AWAY!

THERE'S ONLY ONE THING FOR IT. I'LL HAVE TO GO AFTER THE SHIP ON THIS PRECARIOUS RAFT I HAVE FASHIONED FROM DRIFT-WOOD AND UNDERPANTS!

With a stiff breeze billowing in his breex and using a spare pair as a makeshift and singularly ineffecient paddle, Felix frantically headed towards the distant ship.

I'M GAINING ON HER. SHE DOESN'T SEEM TO BE MOVING.

PANTIE CELESTE

AHOY THERE! ANYONE ABOARD?

79

600 years of aesthetic femininity

FOR CENTURIES, the World's great artists have drawn their inspiration from women's tits. From Leonardo to Picasso, from Rembrandt to Rolf Harris, knockers have been one of the enduring themes to which the creative genius has returned time and again.

Now, the Royal Male invites you to join in celebrating 600 years of churns in art. Our new portfolio of postage stamps features some of the most beautiful and timeless headlamps selected from the greatest paintings in the World's most magnificent collections. They're yours to cherish in the privacy of your own lavatory for years to come.

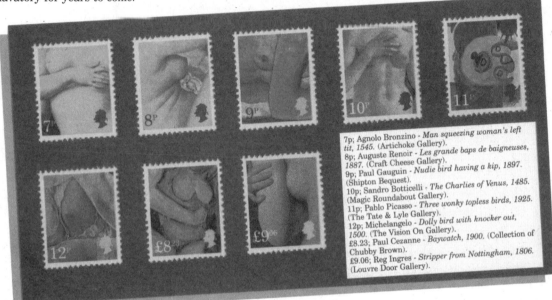

7p; Agnolo Bronzino - *Man squeezing woman's left tit, 1545.* (Artichoke Gallery).
8p; Auguste Renoir - *Les grande baps de baigneuses, 1887.* (Craft Cheese Gallery).
9p; Paul Gauguin - *Nudie bird having a kip, 1897.* (Shipton Bequest).
10p; Sandro Botticelli - *The Charlies of Venus, 1485.* (Magic Roundabout Gallery).
11p; Pablo Picasso - *Three wonky topless birds, 1925.* (The Tate & Lyle Gallery).
12p; Michelangelo - *Dolly bird with knocker out, 1500.* (The Vision On Gallery).
£8.23; Paul Cezanne - *Baywatch, 1900.* (Collection of Chubby Brown).
£9.06; Reg Ingres - *Stripper from Nottingham, 1806.* (Louvre Door Gallery).

Available November 1st from your Post Office,
Newsagent or Mucky Bookshop

AT LAST! It's possible to drive AND ogle in safety, thanks to the
RANDY O'HOPKIRK
REAR VIEW ARSE MIRROR

A BREAKTHROUGH IN OPTICAL TECHNOLOGY!

£5.99

2"

TURNING round to look at a bird's arse whilst driving can be dangerous - and could lead to a cricked neck.
BUT thanks to this revolutionary Italian prismatic attachment, a glance in your wing mirror is all it takes to bring birds' arses into pin-sharp focus.

LEAVES RIGHT ARM FREE FOR OBSCENE GESTURES!

"Now I can ogle birds' arses without turning. Not only is it safer, but Mrs. B of Essex doesn't suspect a thing."

Mr B.,
Essex

Available from HALFORDS and places like that.

"I'm having my daughter trained so she can look after me when my wife dies."

SEND YOUR 6 year-old daughter away to the
THE LONDON COLLEGE
OF BEING A WOMAN

and we'll give you her back in 12 years, fully trained in COOKING, CLEANING, IRONING and HOOVERING UP

NB ~ After 12 years, you may receive a different daughter of equivalent quality to the one originally deposited.

BAZ's LAST STAND

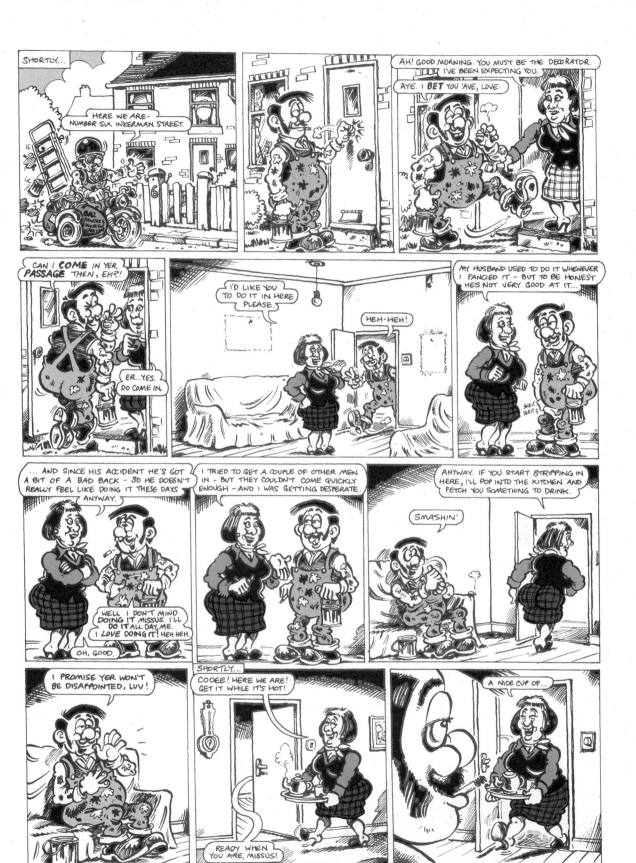

SHRIEK!!

'ERE, WHAT'S GOIN' ON?!

I AIN'T DONE OWT CHIEF, HONEST.

DORIS! ARE YOU ALRIGHT? SPEAK TO ME, DORIS!

DORIS? DORIS? 'OO THE FUCK'S DORIS?

I THOUGHT SHE WAS DOUBLE DECKER LIL, THE TRADESMAN'S FAVOURITE.

DOUBLE DECKER LIL? AH NO, MATE...

THIS IS THE THIRD SCARE POOR DORIS'S HAD THIS WEEK.

SHE'S OVER THE ROAD AT NUMBER SIX — THIS IS NUMBER NINE. IT'S JUST THAT ONE OF THE NAILS FELL OUT THE NUMBER ON THE GATE, SO IT LOOKS LIKE A SIX, SEE.

MIND YOU, IT'S ABOOT TIME WE GOT IT FIXED.

TCHOH.

SHE ASKED THE MILKMAN TO GIVE HER SOME CREAM YESTERDAY...

'TOOK TWO HOURS TO BRING HER ROUND.

THAT'S LIL'S THERE, LOOK. WHERE THE GAS-MAN'S COMING OUT.

OH, RIGHT.

HE READS THAT METER THREE TIMES A WEEK.

89

91

San & Tray's Friday Night Pub Crawl Ga...

Visit the toilet.

Miss a turn.

You pay to go in a nightclub only to find that it is a rave, there is no alcohol on the premises and all the blokes are sweaty, dazed-looking fourteen year olds. **Miss a turn.**

You attempt sex in the pub car park with a casual acquaintance who suffers from premature ejaculation. **Miss a turn** whilst you clean the spunk off your dress.

There is no queue at the chip shop and a fresh batch has just come out of the lard. **Advance 3 squares.**

You have Baz up a ba... and attempt to have s... him. Throw again to s... has brewers dro... Odd Number = Dr... **Move back 2 squa...** Even Number = Pant... **Move forward 2 sq...**

There's a Sambuca promotion on in a pub and you have two pints for the price of one. You feel like you're in a washing machine. **Move forward 3 squares.**

Happy Hour! Three shots for a quid. **Have another turn.**

You are caught short and have to have a piss in a shop doorway and you splash your knickers. **Move back 2 squares.**

You come across some men on a stag night. The groom has drunk 28 pints and is slipping in and out of a coma, but you manage to pull him off. **Move forward 2 squares.**

You lose Baz in a crowded pub and have to buy your own drink. **Move back 4 squares.**

Visit the toilet.

Miss a turn.

You throw violently in back of a t... **Move forw... 2 squares.**

You corner Baz in a bus stop and attempt to have sex with him. Throw again to see if he has brewers droop. Odd Number = Droop. **Move back 2 squares.** Even Number = Panhandle. **Move forward 2 squares.**

You have no money left for a taxi home, so you offer to pay in kind. **Miss a turn** whilst the cabby feels your tits.

Start

Finish

...go for a curry ...d Baz shits ...elf. He throws ...ay his soiled ...sers with his ...allet in the ...ket. YOU have ...y for the meal. ...ck to the start.

Visit the toilet.

Miss a turn.

You are arrested for being drunk and disorderly. **Miss 2 turns** while several policemen gang bang you in the back of a transit van before releasing you with a caution.

The hunk you have spent ten minutes chatting up turns out to be an arse bandit. **Move back 2 squares.**

You wake up in an alleyway with your knickers in your handbag. You have a thumping headache, you do not know where you are, or who you are. **Move forward 4 squares.**

You trap Baz in a 'phone box and attempt to have sex with him. Throw again to see if he has brewers droop.
Odd Number = Droop.
Move back 2 squares.
Even Number = Panhandle.
Move forward 2 squares.

Everybody loves a Friday night piss up. Well now every night can be Friday night with this spectacular Fat Slags Friday night pub crawl game. Simply get two small objects to use as counters, e.g. a button and a sugar cube, roll a dice and away you go. You may like to drink heavily whilst playing the game. The winner is the person who wins.

You avoid paying your bus fare by shagging the conductor, but in doing so, leave an expensive pair of knickers stuffed down the seat. **Stay where you are.**

The doorman at the nightclub lets you in for free after you've pulled him off in the cloakroom. **Move forward 2 squares.**

...order half a ... and lime and ...e barman ...dently gives ...the alcohol-...variety. **Move ...k 2 squares.**

You stagger drunken into the path of a car which screeches to a halt. You bang on the bonnet repeatedly whilst shouting incoherent abuse at the driver before laughing raucously and tottering off.
Move forward 4 squares.

You come across some women on a hen night and in a drunken stupor, you end up wearing the large cardboard hat with condoms on it. **Move back 2 squares.**

Visit the toilet.

Miss a turn.

You discover that a randy barman has been trying to get you pissed by spiking your drinks and you are legless after three halves of lager. **Have another turn.**

FISH N CHIPS

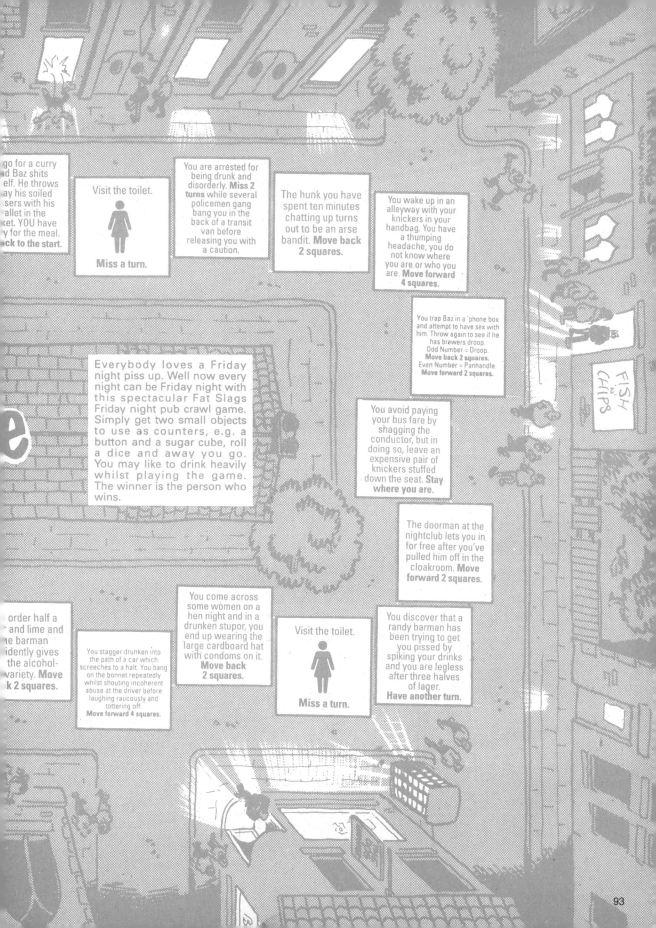

93

Mrs Brady

OLD LADY

PISSY STENCH

TSSCHFTT!

BACK ON THE BUS IN TWENTY MINUTES, LADIES. REMEMBER... TWENTY MINUTES.

THAT'S GOOD, CISSIE. THERE'S JUST TIME TO GET MESELF A NICE PEOPLE'S FRIEND TO READ ON THE BUS.

BUS, YES.

HERE WE ARE...

WANKING HGV DRIVER INTEREST

TSK TSK. THE MORE I SEE, THE MORE DISGUSTED I GET, CISSIE. EEH, THERES A WOMAN HERE AND YOU CAN SEE HER MINNIE MOO. AND THERES NO KNITTING PATTERNS NEITHER. IT'S A DISGRACE.

NEITHER, NO. YES, THAT'S RIGHT.

£2·50.

EEH. I REMEMBER WHEN THE PEOPLE'S FRIEND WAS FOURPENCE HA'PENNY.

YES. IN THEM DAYS YOU COULD GO INTO TOWN WITH HALF A CROWN, GET CLOSE UP PINK INTERNATIONAL, NEW CUNTS AND EUROPEAN CUM BATH...

...AND STILL HAVE A TANNER LEFT FOR YOUR BUS FARE HOME.

PLEASE PAY HERE

COME ON, CISSIE. WE DON'T WANT TO BE LATE. TWENTY MINUTES THE DRIVER SAID.

EEH. HOLD ON. DON'T GO WITHOUT US.

IBIZA EXPRESS

EXIT to M6

94

SHORTLY...

LET US OUT ME SEAT, CISSIE. I'M GOING TO TRY FOR A SIT-DOWN VISIT. I'VE NOT MANAGED A BOB SINCE DOLLY'S FUNERAL, YOU KNOW.

NON STOP IBIZA! EEH. FANCY.

I THINK IT WERE THEM SANDWICHES I HAD AT THE CREMATORIUM. POTTED TONGUE ALLUS BINDS ME UP IN THE BACK-BODY.

WC

WITH ME IT'S THE OPPOSITE, ADA. TONGUE GIVES ME TERRIBLE DIARRHOEA. I'VE BEEN DYING TO TRUMP ALL WEEK ONLY I DARESN'T.

A HOURS LATER...

...EXCUSE ME. IS YOUR FRIEND ALRIGHT? SHE'S BEEN IN THE TOILET FOR AGES.

OOH, YES.

SHE'S TRYING TO DO A MOTION, YOU SEE. SHE'S HAD NO FEESHUS OUT HER ANUS FOR FIVE DAYS, YOU KNOW.

ADA! IT'S ME, CISSIE. ARE YOU ALRIGHT IN THERE?

WC

OOH, YES.

TAP TAP

HOW DID YOU GET ON?

I ONLY MANAGED A COUPLE OF RABBIT TODS.

I'LL TRY AGAIN WHEN WE GET TO BOWNESS.

...EEH WE'VE BEEN ON THIS BUS THREE DAYS, CISSIE. THE LAKES WAS NEVER THIS FAR WHEN I WERE A GIRL.

AYE. IT WAS MUCH NEARER IN THE OLDEN DAYS.

IBIZA QUEEN
BALEARIC FERRIES

LATER...

COME ON, CISSIE. IT'S THIS WAY TO THE BEATRIX POTTER TEA-ROOMS. I JUST FANCY A NICE CUP OF A TEA AND A SCONE.

I CAN'T HAVE SCONES, ME. THE SEEDS IN THE SULTANAS LODGE UNDER ME TOP PLATE AND BRING ME GUMS UP ALL PUS.

WELL... I MIGHT HAVE ONE OR TWO. WITH SOME NICE RASPBERRY JAM.

95

EEH. THAT TAKES ME BACK. THE STEAM GONDOLA TO AMBLESIDE. MY SIDNEY TOOK ME ON THAT WHEN WE WERE COURTING. IT'S WHERE WE FIRST HELD HANDS.

OH, SIDNEY. WHY DID YOU EVER HAVE TO LEAVE HER?

PARA GLIDE

MIND, HOLDING HANDS WAS ALL WE DID. WE WERE VERY INNOCENT IN THEM DAYS.

AYE. THESE DAYS IT'S ALL SNOGGING AND SMOOCHING...

...HAWAIIAN MUSCLE-FUCKS, HOT KARL AND DVDA.

HOW MUCH FOR TWO OAP'S RETURN TO AMBLESIDE?

AND WE'LL BE COUNTING US CHANGE, YOU TURKS.

OW! THAT'S NIPPING ME LISK.

LISK, YES. THAT'S RIGHT.

VOOM!

WOOO OO-OOOOAH!

OOOOAH. YES, THAT'S RIGHT.

OOH, MY GIDDY AUNT.

AC. GPO. 50.DB.SY. 6-00. S.4

SHORTLY...

WHAT HAPPENED THERE, ADA? YOU WAS UP EVER SO HIGH.

I THINK THE DRIVER MUST OF BEEN AND LEFT THE WINDOW OPEN AND HAPPEN I'VE CAUGHT A GUST.

ANY ROAD, THE FRESH AIR'S EASED ME. I FINALLY MANAGED TO SHIFT THAT TONGUE SANDWICH.

OH, I AM PLEASED FOR YOU. THAT DUTY'S BEEN WEIGHING HEAVY ON YOU, HASN'T IT.

COME ON. LET'S FIND TIMOTHY WHITES AND GET YOU SOME HANDY ANDIES.

The End

GEORDIE of UNITED

Miner Geordie Millstone worked 12 hours every day of the week, but Saturday was different, it saw him turn out for his local football team, West Allotment Casuals. Geordie had a dream that one day he would pull on the Black and White shirt of Oldcastle United

One Saturday after a good win for West Allotment...

Excuse me, young man, may I have a word?

I'm Duggie Watson, Oldcastle talent scout. I was very impressed with your performance out there today. Watching you from the terraces I can see you have skills that could take you to a higher level than this. How would you like to turn out for United?

Wow!

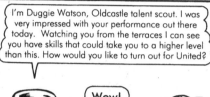

The Black and Whites! How could I say no?

Okay, son. This Saturday. It's the big match against Redchester Rovers. You'll start off on the bench but the boss might put you on for the last ten minutes if you're lucky

Think you can handle it, Son?

I won't let you down, I've lived for this moment

See you Saturday

Down the pit...

Well, Geordie, tomorrow's your big day, lad. Good luck. We'll be watchin' out for you

Aye. I reckon all of West Allotment'll be there

Thanks, lads

Next day...

Hey, Mister!

You're Geordie Millstone, the new signing! Can I have your autograph?

This is like a dream come true!

Shortly...

Right. Today's a big day. **Very** big. We've got to go out there and give a good account of ourselves. We all know what sort of damage Redchester will cause if we don't close them down. They've got a lethal strike force, so stick to your man

Go in **hard**. Go in **strong**. I want **total commitment**. The TV cameras are here, so the whole country will be watching. Go out there and take them apart

Right. Get your boots on. And remember, **enjoy yourselves**

And the Oldcastle trainer is on with the magic sponge... the copper's insisting he's carried off. Oh dear, this looks bad for Thomson...

...Oldcastle only have untried new boy Geordie Millstone on the bench, but they've got no choice. Thomson's afternoon is over. They're warming the lad up

Go on son! **Finish it!** Get it down your neck! Drink lager! **Drink lager!** Go out there! Them Redchester boys...one of them call your mam **a whore!**...

I'll kick their fuckin' heads in!

That's it Son! Keep that spirit up

You're goin' home in a fu-kin' am-bu-lance!

...Oh, and the new boy's straight into the action, showing good use of both feet. He's turned his man **brilliantly**. Tremendous skill!

What a debut! This boy is **unstoppable!** He's taken out five Redchester lads on a 25-terrace solo run with a plywood hoarding! What tenacity...

The police have closed him down, but his talents are amazing. He's managed a 3-coppers' hat-trick on his inauguration...

...and a textbook arrest to cap it off! What a way to open your criminal record! These scenes will surely be remembered as some of the most disgraceful ever seen at this ground!

The next day...

Look, Mum. I've put Oldcastle back on the map! We're out of Europe...thanks to **me!**

I'm so proud of you, Son

OLDCASTLE NEWS
THE UNACCEPTABLE FACE OF FOOTBALL

UNITED BARRED FROM ALL INTERN COMPETITIONS

Epilogue - After an unequalled career of over 800 appearances in court for Oldcastle, and 50 arrests for England, the people of Oldcastle pulled down a statue in Geordie Millstone's honour

SPOILT BASTARD'S BIG TOP ADVENTURE

FEATURING PRINCESS TIFFANY

The Joy of Banging

The internationally best~selling lover's guide to hurried 'no-frills' poking.

By Dr. Baz Comfort M.D, Ph.D, S.T.D (N.S.U.)

The Congress of the Taxi Rank

This is an ideal position for those who have just met in a night club and don't particularly want to see each other again. He shouldn't skimp on the foreplay, asking the people behind to allow him plenty of arse room. She should bend forward slightly, lifting her skirt and bracing herself on the couple in front. He starts thrusting frantically, building up over the next 20 seconds before letting out a couple of pig-like grunts. She should remain non-plussed by his energetic ministrations, occasionally asking other people in the queue what the fuck they're looking at.

Continued over...

Riding the Canon

A good position for those who've had their inhibitions loosened after a few drinks at the office party. He gets her in the mood by drunkenly explaining how his wife doesn't understand him. Both then slip off to the copier room where she unzips his trolleys and pushes him back onto the photocopier. She jumps on top and frantically but vainly bounces on his limp chopper which fails to respond. She should shout his name loud enough for everyone in the office to hear while he makes pathetic, slurred apologies about how this has never happened before. Don't forget the afterplay, which involves five years of eye avoidance and photocopies of his arse and nuts pinned on the office notice board.

The Gentleman's Excuse-me

A convenient position for the sexually impatient couple in a pub. The advantage for her is deep penetration of up to $3\frac{1}{2}$ inches, and comfortable support from the urinal. The advantage for him is that he has already got his charlie out for when he wants to have his post-coital piss. Less extrovert couples may like to use a cubicle for their banging, but check first, as she may be put off by the sight and stench of a cracked bog-pan containing a week's worth of bomb-bay mix.

The Backseat Driver

Confined spaces can be a turn-on for many novelty-hungry couples. She should lie as flat as she can on the back seat of the car and remove her knickers. He should attempt to clamber through the front seats into the back whilst trying to get his kex down far enough to get his wedding tackle out. She should call out "There's a fucking copper coming" to heighten his sense of urgency. When his foreskin is caught securely in his zip, she should attempt to clamber into the driver's seat, sticking her arse in his face in the process, and drive to the nearest casualty department where the nurses will snigger and tell all their mates what has happened.

The Back Passage

A sensual al-fresco position much favoured by those of a shyer nature who require a higher degree of privacy, and those who live at home with their mum. Remember that variety is the spice of life, so don't be afraid to make full use of all the available street furniture ~ dustbins, skips full of rubble and burnt out settees are all grist to the mill of the imaginative fanny rat and hose monster.

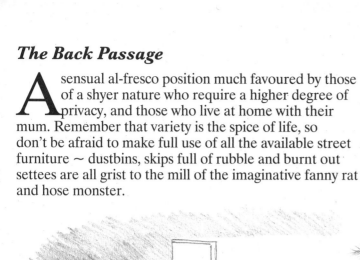

The Pearl & Dean Necklace

The urge to express feelings through physical affection can come upon anyone at any time, and these urges should be indulged whenever possible. In a crowded cinema, however, full penetrative sex is obviously not possible, as the armrests stick up her arse and there is a danger of spilling popcorn. In these situations, a hurried gobble is the ideal way to keep him occupied during the bits between the car chases and the explosions.

The Salt & Vinegar Strokes

A good, hurried bang often involves more than one of our senses, and this position relies heavily on our sense of taste. The woman braces herself against the counter with her left hand, taking care not to burn herself on the hot surface. She then uses her teeth, lips and tongue to playfully tease vast quantities of chips down her neck like a gannet. He lowers his trousers 8 inches, grasps her round the waist and scuttles for all he is worth. He carries on until he reaches orgasm or his haddock is ready. This position has many variations, so don't be afraid to experiment in the kebab shop, the Chinese takeaway, Domino's pizzas ~ *anywhere*.

HOW MANY OF THESE 150 VIZ CHARACTERS CAN YOU RECOGNISE BEFORE IT'S TIME TO WIPE YOUR ARSE, PULL UP YOUR TROUSERS AND LEAVE THE LAVATORY? *Actually, don't bother. Here's the answers: Joe (or occasionally Ti* the assistant, Professor Piehead, Mrs Timpson (Spoilt Bastard's Mum), Joe (Sid's mate), Professor Wolfgang Schnell BSc. PhD., Fatha Bacon, Peter Pretend, Mrs Saunders (Finbarr's mum), Victor Pratt the Stupid Twat, Nobby Piles (or sometimes Giles), Doctor Crapulence, Mrs A (Eight's wife), Doctor Sex, Jethro Palmer, Biffa Bacon, Daley Starr, Tommy Brown, The Antmaster, Maxwell Straker, Tubby Johnson, Baz (another one of Sid's mates), Raffles, Sister Olive, Luvvie Darling, Cilla Blackbeard, Captain Oats, PC Hopper, Dickie Beasley, Grandfather Clo Baxter Basics MP, Bob (Sid's other mate), Tommy Salter, The Brown Bottle, Victorian Dad, Farmer Palmer, Pop Shot, St Bernard Manning, The Duke of Edinburgh, Pre-Menstrual Tensing, Simon Lotion, Mr Gimlet, Ravey Davy Gravy, Ian "It's the way I yell 'em"Paisley, The Folkie, B Connolly, Cowboy Builder, Simon's Snowman, Road Rushdie, Badly Overdrawn Boy, A Thing, Aldridge Prior, Baz Askwith, Ivan Jellical, Fru T Bunn, Segs (not Specs) Maniac, Flash Harry, The Parkie, Norman the Doorman, Billy No-Mates, Tasha Slappa, Lazy Disinterested 16-year- Shoe/Chip/Photo Shop Girl, Napoleon Bonaparte, Emperor Ming, Spoilt Bastard (Timmy Timpson), Sheridan Poorly, Grassy Knollington, Bart Conrad, Gilbert Ratchet, Paul Daniels, Shitty Dick, Stag Knight, Billy Bumblebeard, Old Mother Teresa, Reverend Ramsden, Timothy Pott

...mond Porter, Dick Twitcher, Mutha Bacon, Jump Jet Fanny, Billy Quizz, Mrs Brady, Billy Bananahead, Roger Irrelevant, Garry Bushell the Bear, Morris Stokes Paranormal Grocer, Mr Logic, Norman Norris (Norman's Knob), Roger Mellie, Mickey on his Monkey-Spunk Moped, ...kney Wanker, a Rock'n'Roll Dog Turd, Sid the Sexist, Rodney Rix, Miss Demeanour & her Concertina, Johnny Fartpants, Postman Plod (not Postman Pat, as a number of people put), Tray (Fat Slags), Playtime Fontayne, The Independent Financial Adviser of the Lamp, Yasser ...at (Yasser's Glasses), Major Misunderstanding, Copper Kettle, Felix, Captain Magnetic, Rude Kid, Jack-in-the-Box, Finbarr saunders, Rolf Harris the Cat, A Robo Jobo (from Jimbo Jumbo's Robo Jobos), Big vern, Brown Eye PI, Mickey's Miniature Grandpa, Paul Whicker the Tall ..., Mr Rudewords, Norbert Colon, San (Fat Slags), Tommy and his Magic Arse, Suicidal Syd, Christ - is anybody actually bothering to read this?, Terry Fuckwitt, Tinribs, Billy Bottom, Millie Tant, Victor's Boo Constrictor, Buster Gonad, Balsa Boy, Jelly Head Robertson, A Biscuit ..., Thermos O'Flask, Tom (Roger Mellie's Director), Gordon's Grandad, A Bottom Inspector, Jimmy Hill, Vlad the Impaler, Tommy 'Banana' Johnson, Cardinal Bluto, Pope-Eye, Student Grant, A Pathetic Shark, Careless McKenzie, Albert O'Balsam, Lord Shite, Sergei, Porn Again ...stian, Ben Gunn (Pirates of Ben's Pants), 8 Ace, Shirker Bee, Max Power and Jamie Bond the Schoolboy Spy with Learning Difficulties. Oh, and Invisible Johnny X, so that makes 151.

FROM FLOWER TO TOAST
The Magic of Honey

Honey begins its wondrous journey in the most unlikely of places – a garden. And while the gardener is hard at work, so are the flowers, 24 hours a day, making our favourite breakfast treat.

A flower is like a factory. It takes water from the soil, and sunlight from the sky, and with a little bit of Mother Nature's knowhow, makes it into honey. Now the flower's work is done, and it's time for Mr Bee to take over.

The humble bumble bee is nature's delivery van. His job is to collect honey from the flowers and deliver it safe and sound to a place where it is put in jars. On goes the lid, and the honey is then whisked away to a supermarket shelf – the next stop on it's magical journey.

The honey then makes its final voyage, via mum's grocery basket and onto your kitchen table. Yummy! Spread on hot toast, what a delicious treat! And who'd have thought that only five hours ago that delicious, sticky honey was just a twinkle in Mother Nature's eye.

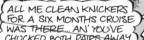

JESUS! THERE'S NOBODY ON THIS SHIP UNDER A HUNDRED.

AYE! IT'S LIKE A FUCKIN' FLOATIN' HOSPICE, TRAY

'OLD ON, THOUGH... LOOK AT THAT SMOKE! I WONDER IF WE'VE BEEN LOOKIN' IN THE RIGHT PLACE

EH?...WHAT D'Y' MEAN?

WELL SMOKE MEANS BOILERS... AN' BOILERS MEANS BOILERMEN... AN' BOILERMEN MEANS BIG MUSCLELY BLOKES WI' HAIRY ARSES!

WHAT ARE WE WAITIN' FOR?

SO...

HEH! HEH!

TO ENGINE ROOM
AUTHORISED PERSONNEL ONLY

NOW WE'LL USE ALL US FEMININE CHARMS ON 'EM, SAN. THEY WON'T BE ABLE TO RESIST US SUBTLE FLIRTATIONS...

ENGINE ROOM

COO-EE! ANYBODY FANCY A FUCK?

...I'M AS WET AS AN OTTER'S POCKET

AYUP, LADS. A COUPLE MORE BOILERS FOR US TO STOKE, EH?

SHORTLY...

GREAT SCOTT! THERE'S AN ICEBERG...DEAD AHEAD, CAPTAIN.

BRIDGE TO ENGINE ROOM...REVERSE ENGINES...REVERSE ENGINES.

CAPTAIN TO ENGINE ROOM... REVERSE ENGINES NOW!

THEY'RE NOT RESPONDING

Your Medical Questions Answered

Dr. Sidney Smutt

Dear Dr. Smutt,
How much fags is it safe to smoke?
Frank.
Walford

Dr. Smutt replies
It is safe to smoke upwards of 80 or 100 tabs a day. My grandad smoked 270 a day from the age of six, and he was killed running for a bus when he was 104. His brother, who did'nt never smoke was ran over by a bus when he was 28.

Dr. Smutt is a proper doctor and knows what he's on about

For everyone life is difficult sometimes. But for people like Stanley it's difficult *all* the time.

For people like Stanley (not his real name) a trip to the shop (it's Sidney) to buy some tabs can turn into a nightmare. An evening at the pub often ends in an ambulance trip to hospital. Taking a girl to the cinema will almost certainly end in him being kicked in the pods. Society shuns him, people avoid him in the street.

Because, through no fault of his own, Stanley is a twat.

Shortly after his birth, he began showing the first signs of the dismal personality which now leaves him a sad and pathetic laughing-stock amongst his peers and, more importantly to Stanley, deeply repellent to women.

Because of his boorish, unpleasant behaviour, no self-respecting woman would touch him with a bargepole. There is nothing that can be done to change his personality and give him a chance of scoring. The future is bleak. As he gets older, he'll simply become more of a twat. Deep down he knows he'll never break his duck.

But you can help make Stanley's life more bearable:

£1 will buy him a week's viewing of the Fantasy Channel on Satellite
£5 will buy a glossy top shelf scud mag and a box of man-size tissues
£10 will buy a copy of Sluts International on VHS
£15 will pay for a three minute phone call to a sex line terminating in Ulan Bator
£50 will get him a deeply regrettable blow job off a woman in a pub car park

Think about people like Stanley when you're on the job. And please help

Fuck off. I'm not giving any money to twats like that. ☐ I enclose nowt.
Signed.........................Name ....
Address..
Send to: Sexist Appeal. FREEPOST. Leeds

Less than 98% of the money we raise is eaten up by administration and the staff Christmas party.

Tired of being slapped in the face by women for your suggestive comments? *Then rise above them!*

Jeer-Stage
SECTIONAL HARASSMENT PLATFORM

Only £199.99

Now it's easy to shout at and embarrass women in complete safety without the danger of redress with the JEER-STAGE. Easily erected, the four storey scaffold, available for the first time to the amateur allows **professional quality** verbal assault to be achieved from even the novice DIY builder or handyman.

Each JEER-STAGE comes complete with a hard hat and phrase book of the most coarse insults and wolf calls used on today's building sites.

Please rush me one of those four-storey JEER-STAGE things.
I enclose £...............
Name..........Address......................

JEER-STAGE Ltd,
PO Box 1. Hull.

You'll never feel clean again
after a stay at the
TIPTON SHAGNASTY HOTEL

THE SHAGNASTY HOTEL, nestling in the heart of the West Midlands provides the perfect hideaway for a sordid hour frantically poking that special someone you've just picked up. At the Tipton Shagnasty, we boast:

* PAPER THIN WALLS * MAPS OF AFRICA ON ALL BED LINEN *
* THIEVING STAFF * SMELL OF PISS THROUGHOUT *
* HAPPY HOUR OVERCHARGING AT THE BAR *
* RAT SHIT * NO ROOM SERVICE *

40 imaginatively appointed bedroom suites, crammed into a standard two bedroomed end terraced house. A single room costs from as little as 50p a minute for two people. There's no reservations necessary so come stay with us and get away from it all for 15 minutes or so.

Fulchester Joint Matriculation Board

GCE Ordinary Level Examination Paper

Sexism Studies

A stiflingly hot afternoon, June, 1980
time allowed 3 hrs

Attempt all questions. If you do not know the answer to a particular question, attempt to look at someone else's paper by knocking your biro onto the floor and having a shufty while you lean over to retrieve it. You are allowed one visit to the toilet to look at the answers you wrote on the wall yesterday. After ten minutes, request more paper to shit up the other candidates into thinking that you must have wrote loads. Attempt to introduce the one or two facts you are reasonably sure of into the answers to every question. At 4.30 exactly, everybody cough to make the invigilator jump. With three minutes to go, suddenly realise there are 4 more questions on the back of the page that you haven't spotted. You are going to fail.

Section A (20%)

1. Explain why the best women's football team in the world wouldn't stand a chance against you and ten of your mates. Include in your answer
    a) why they are unable to kick a ball straight
    b) what you wouldn't mind doing with them in the bath after the match, though.

2. Pamela Anderson's tits are plastic but look good in photographs. Compare and contrast the relative merits of plastic and real tits for recreational purposes.

3. It is a long established fact that fat lasses are more grateful for it. Outline some of the reasons why this is so, and explain why all feminists are fat, ugly lesbians.

4. Write a critique of any ONE of the following films you will have watched at your mates house while his parents were away for the weekend.
    a) Sex Boat
    b) Three Into One Will Go
    c) King Dong
    d) Speared by Zulu Lovers

5. Women drivers, eh? Discuss.

Section B (20%)

1. Describe an experiment to impress a girl by lighting a fart. What apparatus would you require? What risks would you run in lighting a fart and what are the benefits? Write a balanced chemical equation to describe the reaction that takes place when an eggy fart is lit in a pub with a match.

2. Explain, using diagrams if necessary, how it is possible to tell if a woman is a virgin or not from the way she walks.

3. Name something a woman has invented.

4. Argue heatedly over the respective merits of the Lambourghinni Diablo and the Ferrari Testerossa without ever having seen, let alone driven, either.

5. On average, women live 7 years longer than men yet get their pension 5 years earlier. Explain why this isn't fair, making reference to your lazy old granny who lived to be 100 and your poor grandad who worked 52 years down the pit and died the day before he retired.

CIRCUS

BILLY SMART'S

PRINCESS MARINA
Tightrope Walker

Look up and gasp as she treads the high wire 50 feet above the ring- without the aid of knickers!

OLAF THE FEARLESS
Lion tamer

Shows no fear as he puts his wife's head into a lion's

BERT TWO RIVERS
Red Indian Dinner Thrower

Hold your breath as he comes in from the pub and throws his burnt dinner at his wife

FEARLESS FREDA
Lady Spider Tamer

You'll not believe your eyes as she takes quite a big spider out the bath- armed only with a glass and a birthday card

The World Famous

they're been drinking since breakfast

STROMBOLI the MIGHTY

Gets the lid off the tomato sauce for his wife—without using the doorframe

THE AMAZING KEITH

Traditional Plate Washing Act

Gasp as Keith's missus washes 40 plates simultaneously—while he has a cup of tea

ALFREDO GAZPACCI

Scooter Stuntman

Thrill as he rides blindfold round the ring pinching 60 birds on the arse

Plus the

BILLY SMUTT BIG TOP SHOWGIRLS

They can't sing, they can't dance, but they've got massive tits

APPEARING ALL THIS WEEK AT:

A FIELD KNEE DEEP IN MUD AND ELEPHANT SHIT

121

SID the SEXIST
DOON the SMURK

MORE FOUL-MOUTHED FUNNIES WITH YOUR FOUR-LETTER FRIENDS

... SHARON STALLURNE, SHE'S BEIN' QUESTIONED BY THE COPPAZ, AN' SHE KEEPS CROSSIN' HER LEGS, AN SHE'S GOT NEE KNICKAZ ON, Y'CAN SEE HER MUFF, THE LOT!... FUCK ME! WHAT AN ACTRESS!

HOW, LOOK! BAZ, IT'S YOUR DAVE.

OH, AYE! HE MUST'VE JUST GOT BACK FROM LONDON. HE'S BEEN DOON ON THE SITES FOR TWO MONTHS.

HOW, DAVE! ROY! BACK AWA THE TOON, EH?

AYE, SID. THERE'S NOWT LIKE COMIN' AWA THE BRIDGE.

AYE!

MIND, IT'S YOUR ROOND, THOUGH, BUT...

... TWO MONTH ON THE SITES... Y'MUST BE FUCKIN' HEAVIN' WI' SPONDS.

FUCK THAT! I HAVEN'T GOT TWO HA'PENNIES T' RUB TOGETHER.

EH? BUT I THOUGHT THEM JOBS WAS CASH IN HAND.

OH, AYE. CASH IN HAND AALREET...

... IT WUZ IN ME HAND, THEN ME BAALLS SEEN THAT IT WENT STRITE OOT THE END O' ME OLD MAN.

WHADDAYA MEAN, LIKE?

WELL, THERE'S ME AN' SIX OTHER GEORDIES AALL SHACKED UP IN THIS FUCKIN' CARAVAN ON THE SITE. WE TRIED GANNIN' TU THE PUBS, BUT THE FUCKIN' BEER'S AAFUL, AN' IT TOOK ABOOT TWO 'COAZ T' GET A ROOND IN.

Y'SEE, THEY CANNAT UNDASTAND A WORD YE SAY. IT WUZ FUCKIN' DIRE. WE JUST SAT AROOND THE CARAVAN, NEE TELLY OR NOWT. MIND, ONE O' THE LADS HAD KER-PLUNK.

I TELL YUZ, I WAS IN FUCKIN' TEARS AFTER A WEEK. I WENT TU THE PHURN BOX TU CAALL ME MAM, ONLY WHEN I GOT THERE...

... THERE WAS AALL THESE CARDS AALL AWA THE WAALL.

FUCK ME!!

TOO FUCKIN' RIGHT, SID! THAT'S WHAT I THOUGHT. SUR I RANG A ONE UP.

ROXANNE Ring Me on 0171 723 181 FOR A BLUE THESE DREAMS

I AM A CITY

SHE WAS FUCKIN' NECTAR! SUR I GANS WITH ANOTHER ONE THE NEXT NEET. NEXT THING I KNAA, I CANNAT FUCKIN' STOP MESEL'. EVERY FUCKIN' NEET I WUZ HUMPIN'...

... TWICE OF A SATURDUR.

LAYIN' BRICKS OF A DAYTIME, LAYIN' LASSES ON A NIGHT TIME. IT'S A MIRACLE I NEVER PEGGED IT.

FUCKIN' HELL.

ME FUCKIN' BUILDING POOND WAS GERRIN' DEMOLISHED AS FAST AS I MADE THE CUNT.

'ERE, WOT'S 'APPENED T'YAW BLOKE THEN EH? FIFTEEN MILLION HE COST YA, AN' WOT'S 'E DAN? EH? FACK AWL, THAT'S WOT. TWO LEFT FEET 'E'S GOT, FACKIN' WABBISH. MIND YOU, 'E 'AD T'GET RID O' THAT COLE GEEZAH. I MEAN, I'M NO RACIST, BAT HE...

BLAAAR!!

FACK OFF AAHT OF IT!

SCREEECH!

AN HOUR LATER... ...AN' THE FING IS, SHE'S STILL GOT AWL 'ER OWN TEEF. AN' SHE WAS 'ERE AWL FREW THE DARK DAYS OF THE BLITZ, SHE WAS, DODGIN' BLADDY DOODLEBAGS, NOT LIKE THAT FIWFY NORVERN TRAITER GRACIE WOTS'ER-BLADDY-NAME, GOIN' SWANNIN' OFF T'CAPRI TILL IT WAS AWL OVER...

PARP!

GERTCHA!

ANOTHER HOUR LATER... ...AN / SEZ / SHOULD FACKIN' COCOA. BAT IT'S THESE FACKIN' MURDERERS THAT GET ME, I MEAN THEY DO A MURDER AN' GET PUT IN THE NICK AN' IT'S LIKE THE FACKIN' RITZ. I MEAN, I'D 'ANG 'EM I WOULD, I'D DO IT. I'D PULL THE FACKIN' LEVER MESENF... FINK TWICE ABAAHT DOIN' ANAVVER MURDER THEN, THEY WOULD.

NEARLY THERE, CHIEF.

WELCOME TO BRIGHTON

ANOTHER HOUR LATER... ...GOT RID O' NATIONAL SERVICE THEY SHOULDN'T. I RECKON EVERYONE 'OO'S 18 SHOULD DO TWO YEARS NATIONAL SERVICE F'QUEEN AN' CANTRY. AP AT SIX, SQUARE BASHIN', SHININ' YER BOOTS WIV A SPOON. THAT'D SAWT 'EM AAHT. NEVER DID ME ANY 'ARM. MIND YOU, I DIDN'T DO IT, ON ACCAHNT OF ME FEET BEIN' FLAT, Y'SEE...

ZZZZZ

AND ANOTHER... ...BAT THE REAL TRABBLE WIV THE YOOF OF TODAY IS, THAT THEY AIN'T GOT NO RESPECT FOR THE OWLD FOLKS, THEIR ELDERS AN' BETTERS, 'CAUSE THEY JAST DON'T...

BLAAAAR!

GET YER FACKIN' EYES TESTED, GRANDAD!!

GAW! WOT ARE THEY LIKE, EH, SAM OF 'EM? MIND YOU, YOU'LL NEVER GUESS 'OO I 'AD IN THE BACK O' THIS TAXI LARST WEEK. NAAAH, GAW ON, 'AVE A GUESS...

...OOOH! 'ERE WE ARE, MATE. SOHO.

RIGHT THEN, LET'S 'AVE A BUTCHER'S... THAT'S TWO 'ANDRED AN' NINETY QUID PLEASE, JOHN, SORRY ABAAHT. TRAFFIC'S BLADDY MURDER, INNIT?

HEH! HEH! HEH! FANKS A FACKIN' BANCH. YER BLEEDIN' NORVERN PONCE!

VRDOOOM!

PEEP SHOW

XXX CIN

spake unto him out of the window in a voice of thunder saying, Begone 8 Ace who is begat of 32 Eiger.

34 And he took up his tins and dwelt in his shed.

CHAPTER 14.

AND it came to pass that on the seventh day there came from the North East Sidney, who was begat of his mam who dwelt in the land of Byker.

2 And he came down unto the town of New Castle to go to the pub to seek his friends.

3 And he came upon Joe who is begat of Big Joe and Bob and Barry, who is called Baz. And they looked upon their glasses and saw that they were barren. And Sidney was cast forth unto the bar that they be replenished even unto the fourth pint. For it was written that it was His shout.

4 And Sidney did buy the round and some crisps of salt and vinegar and cheeses and onions and the scratchings of the swine of the fields, even unto two bags. And the others who were gathered looked upon the round and they saw that it was good.

5 So they sat back and did drink deeply of the lagers and were becalmed. And they began to cast their lecherous eyes upon the women of the pub and they were tempted for they had fashioned their garments one cubit above the knee and did leave little to the imagination, I can tell you.

6 And their heads were full of unclean thoughts. And Sidney beheld a woman's jugs and did covet them for they were indeed smashing. And he nudged Barry who is called Baz and passed adulterous comment and blasphemed saying he wouldn't mind a faceful of them.

7 But Baz did mock him, saying that he was virgin and chaste and celibate, and that he hath known not a woman though be he one score and eight.

8 Yet did Sidney answer and spake unto those who sat with him, saying these words were untrue, and that the women he hath known were multitude and numbered more than the lilies of the field or the birds of the air.

9 But his friends laughed and reproached him saying, cease with these falsehoods, Sidney, for we are wise to your ways. And they accused him saying that he did take up the Freeman's catalogue and seek the bra pages and spill his seed upon the ground. And they pointed at him and sang cherry boy, cherry boy.

10 And Sidney rose up and great was his anger.

11 And he rebuked them in an terrible voice, saying that they were all a bunch of cunts. But yet did they mock him and great was his woe for he knew in his heart that it was true

12 And in his wrath he did spill the pint of Dave, who is called Mental who sat at the table on his right hand and his pint was cast upon the sticky carpet. And Mental who had a head of skin looked upon it and great was his displeasure. And Sidney spake to him amiable; Behold, for I want not any trouble. But Mental had got the mist, and lo, the mist was red. And he smiled not upon Sidney, but smote him an mighty blow in the teeth.

13 And again.

14 And thrice did he lamp Sidney whose fall was as that of a sack of spuds and great was his suffering.

15 And they heared the voice of the LANDLORD standing behind the bar. And he was sore vexed and spake unto them in a loud voice saying, Yeez lot, oot.

16 And Sidney and Joe who is begat of Big Joe and Bob and Barry who is called Baz were cast out into the car park. And there was much cursing of the name of Sidney and much gnashing of teeth and they wished pestilence upon his head.

CHAPTER 15.

AND it came to pass that after holding counsel they did reach a covenant that they maketh their passage to the house of Ke-Bab, by the bus station. And so they did.

2 And they entered the house. And they looked upon the kebab revolving on the altar and did ask of themselves what was in it.

3 And Baz spoke saying that it was made of the nads and the lips and eyelids of the goat and the cow and the sheep and the cat and all the unclean parts thereof, even unto the chopper and ringpiece.

4 And great was the plague of flies upon the kebab. And the price of the kebabs was one pound and nine and ninety.

5 And Sidney and Joe who is begat of Big Joe and Bob and Barry who is called Baz spoke saying, Four kebabs pal. And the shopkeeper was called Stavros.

6 And Stavros said, Seven pound and six and ninety, matey peeps. And he began preparations for their feast and he did scratch his nuts and take the unleavened bread.

7 And Sidney spoke another parable unto his three disciples; Verily I say unto you, That Dave who is called Mental was geet lucky, for had the LANDLORD not stepped in, yea would I surely have slain the baldy fucker.

8 And they heared a voice and the voice said, Oh yeah? And they turned about them and beheld Dave who is called Mental, for he had likewise journeyed to the house of Ke-Bab.

9 And Sidney's raiments of Levi became besoiled.

10 And he spoke another parable saying; Hello Dave who is called Mental. I was just talking about another Dave who is called Mental.

11 But Dave who is called Mental believed not Sidney's falsehood and great was his wrath.

12 And mighty was the smoting that Sidney took up the bracket and elsewise. And Joe who is begat of Big Joe and Bob and Barry who is called Baz stepped not in for Sidney, but did look at their footwear. They denied Sidney and He was forsaken.

CHAPTER 16.

AND it came to pass that Sidney was put upon a litter. And Joe who is begat of Big Joe and Bob and Barry who is called Baz did journey with him to the land of the Royal General Infirmary, whereupon

8,238,622

CRICKET *in other*

"There isn't a more British scene, than a match of cricket 'pon village green". So wrote Wordsworth in 1744. But nowadays the popularity of our national sport has spread, and the game is enjoyed in the furthest flung corners of the globe, by chaps of every race, religion and colour. For not only has the British Empire been responsible for the spread of fairplay, correct pronounciation and good table manners across the globe, it has also taken with it that unmistakable sound of leather on willow. Yet, whilst cricket is the same game the whole world over, the rules, the object of the game and the way it is played differ greatly from nation to nation.

The frozen wastes of Iceland would be the last place you'd expect to find a game of cricket. But visit any igloo village on a Sunday afternoon and that's exactly what you'll see.

However, look closely and you may spot a few subtle differences from the English game. The Eskimo batsmen, for example, would not wield a willow bat. A large frozen fish has to suffice, for there are no trees in Iceland. As his innings proceeds the fish becomes softer, and scoring runs more difficult. Fielders must beware of holes in the ice, and marauding polar bears attracted by the smell of the bat. Running between wickets is made easier by the use of skis, however many collisions occur as cricket whites often become invisible in Iceland's blizzard weather conditions.

Cricket in the land of the rising sun is more than just a game, it's a matter of honour. Indeed, seldom does a game take place in Japan without at least two ritual suicides on the field of play. Such apparently minor matters as a dropped catch or the bowling of a wide is all that is required to prompt the highly strung oriental sportsmen to disembowel himself with the razor sharp ceremonial cricket sabre, which the umpire carries at all times. The ultimate disgrace is for the batsmen to be out without scoring. Rather than face the humiliating walk back to the bamboo pavilion he will impale himself on his own stumps.

Despite this frequent loss of life, Japan is one of the most densely populated countries in the world. As a consequence their cricket pitches rarely measure more than ten yards square.

lands

Take a trip to the Belgian Congo and you might well expect to see the Pygmy population playing some silly French game or other. But you'd be wrong. For cricket was introduced to these little fellows in 1815 by a group of M.C.C. missionaries from Trent Bridge, and it has been played there religiously ever since. Depsite an average height of only one foot five inches, the Pygmies were determined to enjoy to the full their new found game, regularly organising five-day test matches against teams from neighbouring tribes. Such was their enthusiasm for the sport that in 1894 the Pygmies clubbed together and raised the royal sum of eighteen shillings, enough to pay for the celebrated English cricketer W. G. Grace to come to the Congo for a three week intensive training visit. Unfortunately, whilst demonstrating a forward defensive prod the good doctor accidently trod on the chief of the tribe, killing the tiny fellow outright. Grace was forced to make a hasty exit, pursued by four hundred thousand spear-wielding midgets.

It is a little known fact that during the late 1930's the Government of Norway decreed that cricket was to become their national sport. Many obstacles had to be overcome, not least of which was the complete lack of any space on which to build a pitch. To solve this problem the Government spent £138,000,000 felling every last tree in Norway, and using them to build vast floating 'pontoon' cricket pitches in the fjords. However, the plan was a disasterous failure, as due to an oversight on the part of the Norwegian Minister for National Sport, the cricket season coincided exactly with Norway's winter – the six months of the year when, due to its northerly latitude, the country is plunged into total darkness. One game optimistically started in Trondheim, and Prime Minister Olaf Jurgensen ceremonially tossed the coin to decide which team should bat first. However, in the darkness the umpire was unable to find where the coin had landed, and after several hours of fruitless searching the game was abandoned. Within a week the national sport of Norway had been changed to table tennis.

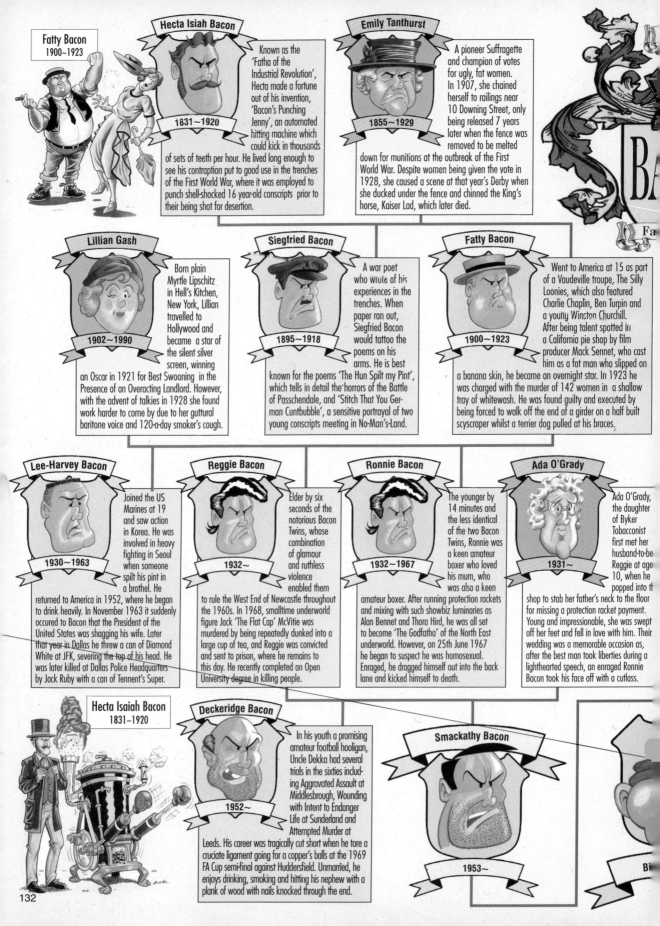

Fatty Bacon
1900~1923

Hecta Isiah Bacon
1831~1920

Known as the 'Fatha of the Industrial Revolution', Hecta made a fortune out of his invention, 'Bacon's Punching Jenny', an automated hitting machine which could kick in thousands of sets of teeth per hour. He lived long enough to see his contraption put to good use in the trenches of the First World War, where it was employed to punch shell-shocked 16 year-old conscripts prior to their being shot for desertion.

Emily Tanthurst
1855~1929

A pioneer Suffragette and champion of votes for ugly, fat women. In 1907, she chained herself to railings near 10 Downing Street, only being released 7 years later when the fence was removed to be melted down for munitions at the outbreak of the First World War. Despite women being given the vote in 1928, she caused a scene at that year's Derby when she ducked under the fence and chinned the King's horse, Kaiser Lad, which later died.

Lillian Gash
1902~1990

Born plain Myrtle Lipschitz in Hell's Kitchen, New York, Lillian travelled to Hollywood and became a star of the silent silver screen, winning an Oscar in 1921 for Best Swooning in the Presence of an Overacting Landlord. However, with the advent of talkies in 1928 she found work harder to come by due to her guttural baritone voice and 120-a-day smoker's cough.

Siegfried Bacon
1895~1918

A war poet who wrote of his experiences in the trenches. When paper ran out, Siegfried Bacon would tattoo the poems on his arms. He is best known for the poems 'The Hun Spilt my Pint', which tells in detail the horrors of the Battle of Passchendale, and 'Stitch That You German Cuntbubble', a sensitive portrayal of two young conscripts meeting in No-Man's-Land.

Fatty Bacon
1900~1923

Went to America at 15 as part of a Vaudeville troupe, The Silly Loonies, which also featured Charlie Chaplin, Ben Turpin and a young Winston Churchill. After being talent spotted in a California pie shop by film producer Mack Sennet, who cast him as a fat man who slipped on a banana skin, he became an overnight star. In 1923 he was charged with the murder of 142 women in a shallow tray of whitewash. He was found guilty and executed by being forced to walk off the end of a girder on a half built scyscraper whilst a terrier dog pulled at his braces.

Lee-Harvey Bacon
1930~1963

Joined the US Marines at 19 and saw action in Korea. He was involved in heavy fighting in Seoul when someone spilt his pint in a brothel. He returned to America in 1952, where he began to drink heavily. In November 1963 it suddenly occured to Bacon that the President of the United States was shagging his wife. Later that year in Dallas he threw a can of Diamond White at JFK, severing the top of his head. He was later killed at Dallas Police Headquarters by Jack Ruby with a can of Tennent's Super.

Reggie Bacon
1932~

Elder by six seconds of the notorious Bacon Twins, whose combination of glamour and ruthless violence enabled them to rule the West End of Newcastle throughout the 1960s. In 1968, smalltime underworld figure Jack 'The Flat Cap' McVitie was murdered by being repeatedly dunked into a large cup of tea, and Reggie was convicted and sent to prison, where he remains to this day. He recently completed an Open University degree in killing people.

Ronnie Bacon
1932~1967

The younger by 14 minutes and the less identical of the two Bacon Twins, Ronnie was a keen amateur boxer who loved his mum, who was also a keen amateur boxer. After running protection rackets and mixing with such showbiz luminaries as Alan Bennet and Thora Hird, he was all set to become 'The Godfatha' of the North East underworld. However, on 25th June 1967 he began to suspect he was homosexual. Enraged, he dragged himself out into the back lane and kicked himself to death.

Ada O'Grady
1931~

Ada O'Grady, the daughter of Byker Tobacconist first met her husband-to-be Reggie at age 10, when he popped into the shop to stab her father's neck to the floor for missing a protection racket payment. Young and impressionable, she was swept off her feet and fell in love with him. Their wedding was a memorable occasion as, after the best man took liberties during a lighthearted speech, an enraged Ronnie Bacon took his face off with a cutlass.

Hecta Isaiah Bacon
1831~1920

Deckeridge Bacon
1952~

In his youth a promising amateur football hooligan, Uncle Dekka had several trials in the sixties including Aggravated Assault at Middlesbrough, Wounding with Intent to Endanger Life at Sunderland and Attempted Murder at Leeds. His career was tragically cut short when he tore a cruciate ligament going for a copper's balls at the 1969 FA Cup semi-final against Huddersfield. Unmarried, he enjoys drinking, smoking and hitting his nephew with a plank of wood with nails knocked through the end.

Smackathy Bacon
1953~

Bi

Fa

BA

Ducker Mellaz
1888~1932

Whippet keeper to Sir Charles Batterley of Scotswood Hall. A strong, quiet man who lived in a small shed next to the kennels of the Scotswood Hall Estate. He was dismissed after Sir Charles caught him and Lady Batterley romping naked around the grounds with daisies plaited in their pubes.

Lady Fanny Batterley
1892~1940

Wife of Sir Charles Batterley of Scotswood Hall, who was shot through both knackers at the Seige of Mafeking. She was thrown out when, having failed to to get sexual satisfaction from her husband, she turned to Mellaz the whippet keeper. They later married and bred Mickey the Miller, the champion whippet of 1923.

Francis Merrick
1932~1996

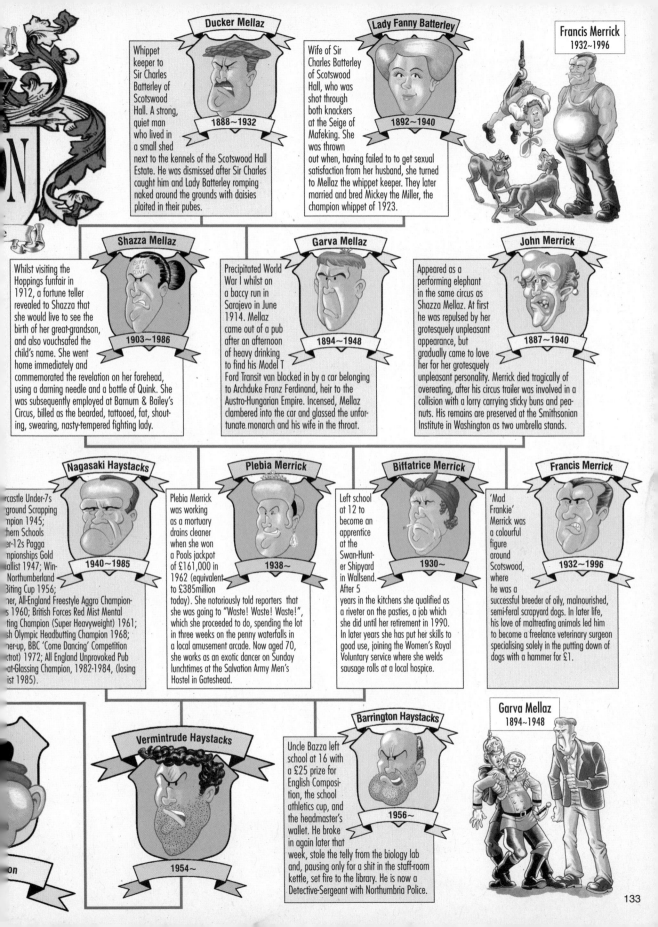

Shazza Mellaz
1903~1986

Whilst visiting the Hoppings funfair in 1912, a fortune teller revealed to Shazza that she would live to see the birth of her great-grandson, and also vouchsafed the child's name. She went home immediately and commemorated the revelation on her forehead, using a darning needle and a bottle of Quink. She was subsequently employed at Barnum & Bailey's Circus, billed as the bearded, tattooed, fat, shouting, swearing, nasty-tempered fighting lady.

Garva Mellaz
1894~1948

Precipitated World War I whilst on a baccy run in Sarajevo in June 1914. Mellaz came out of a pub after an afternoon of heavy drinking to find his Model T Ford Transit van blocked in by a car belonging to Archduke Franz Ferdinand, heir to the Austro-Hungarian Empire. Incensed, Mellaz clambered into the car and glassed the unfortunate monarch and his wife in the throat.

John Merrick
1887~1940

Appeared as a performing elephant in the same circus as Shazza Mellaz. At first he was repulsed by her grotesquely unpleasant appearance, but gradually came to love her for her grotesquely unpleasant personality. Merrick died tragically of overeating, after his circus trailer was involved in a collision with a lorry carrying sticky buns and peanuts. His remains are preserved at the Smithsonian Institute in Washington as two umbrella stands.

Nagasaki Haystacks
1940~1985

...castle Under-7s ...ground Scrapping ...mpion 1945; ...hern Schools ...er-12s Pagga ...mpionships Gold ...allist 1947; Win- ...Northumberland ...Biting Cup 1956; ...ner, All-England Freestyle Aggro Champion-s 1960; British Forces Red Mist Mental ...ting Champion (Super Heavyweight) 1961; ...sh Olympic Headbutting Champion 1968; ...ner-up, BBC 'Come Dancing' Competition ...xtrot) 1972; All England Unprovoked Pub ...at-Glassing Champion, 1982-1984, (losing ...ist 1985).

Plebia Merrick
1938~

Plebia Merrick was working as a mortuary drains cleaner when she won a Pools jackpot of £161,000 in 1962 (equivalent to £385million today). She notoriously told reporters that she was going to "Waste! Waste! Waste!", which she proceeded to do, spending the lot in three weeks on the penny waterfalls in a local amusement arcade. Now aged 70, she works as an exotic dancer on Sunday lunchtimes at the Salvation Army Men's Hostel in Gateshead.

Biffatrice Merrick
1930~

Left school at 12 to become an apprentice at the Swan-Hunter Shipyard in Wallsend. After 5 years in the kitchens she qualified as a riveter on the pasties, a job which she did until her retirement in 1990. In later years she has put her skills to good use, joining the Women's Royal Voluntary service where she welds sausage rolls at a local hospice.

Francis Merrick
1932~1996

'Mad Frankie' Merrick was a colourful figure around Scotswood, where he was a successful breeder of oily, malnourished, semi-feral scrapyard dogs. In later life, his love of maltreating animals led him to become a freelance veterinary surgeon specialising solely in the putting down of dogs with a hammer for £1.

Vermintrude Haystacks
1954~

Barrington Haystacks
1956~

Uncle Bazza left school at 16 with a £25 prize for English Composition, the school athletics cup, and the headmaster's wallet. He broke in again later that week, stole the telly from the biology lab and, pausing only for a shit in the staff-room kettle, set fire to the library. He is now a Detective-Sergeant with Northumbria Police.

Garva Mellaz
1894~1948

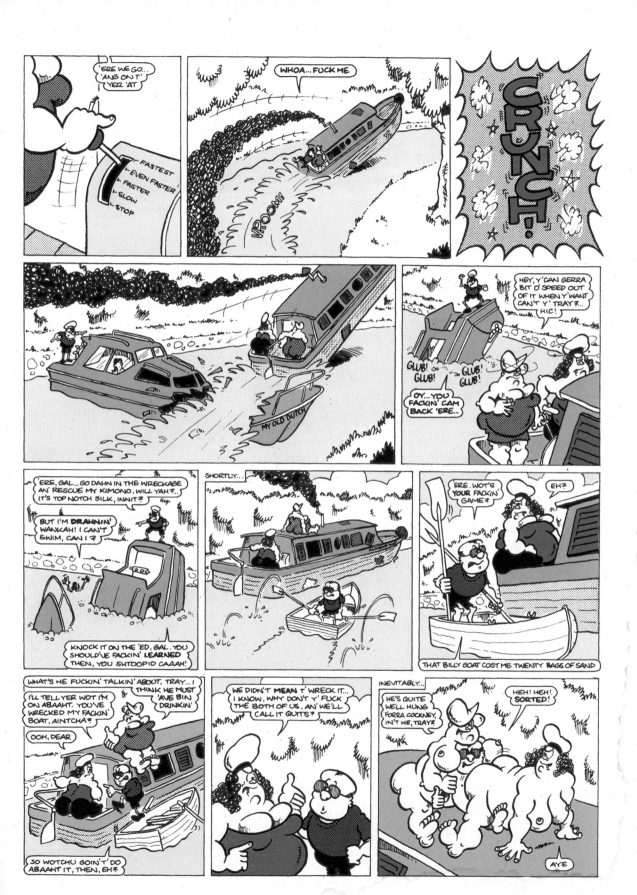

141

"There she blows. A couple of beauties off the starboard bow"

"Ready... aim..."

"Wait... They're not whales... they've got tits... it's a couple of fat English birds"

"Nevermind whale meat for tea... It's a fish supper for everyone. Heh heh heh!"
"Yes"

"I hope this jib takes the strain. It was only designed for smaller whales"

Fighting with

inosaurs

PLACE: The banks of the River Tyne. Huge aggressive monsters with brains no bigger than walnuts indulge in violent battles over territory and the best spot at the watering hole. But what was it like a million years ago?

Geological records show that Tyneside was a very different place, dense with tropical forests, enormous tree ferns and all volcanoes going off and that. And from fossils recently unearthed in a Scotswood allotment, scientists have identified and named five hitherto unknown species of dinosaur. These beasts lived in the North East for about a hundred thousand years, but died out after refusing to wear coats during the Ice Age.

1 *Fathasaurus rex* The biggest and most aggressive carnivore ever to walk the planet. Easily capable of taking on and chinning three big velociraptors without anyone jumping in for it, these ferocious predators could grow to the size of a double decker bus and weigh up to eight tons. Seen here lamping a young biffasaurus for spilling its primordial soup.

2 *Biffasaurus* A carnivorous dinosaur with a distinctive 'woolly hat' shaped bony protruberance on its forehead. It had very loose fitting but quick growing teeth, which meant it could be twatted on a regular basis. It preyed mainly on the softisaurus, but spent most of its time hiding from the larger predators which would often ambush it from behind small ferns and kick its head in.

3 *Softisaurus cedricus* Perhaps the puniest and wimpiest of all the giant reptiles. Often beaten up by the biffasaurus whilst picking flowers with its limp-wristed forelimbs. Even the adults of this timid species were picked on and frightened by biffasaurus, making them cry. Their skin was very thin which made them susceptible to Chinese burns.

4 *Muthaplodicus* Unlike many other saurapodamorphs (eg. Diplodicus, Brachiosaurus and the Apatasuaurs) which were placid vegetarians, the Muthaplodicus were extremely foul-mouthed and aggressive meat-eaters. Living in huge herds scouring swamps of Jurassic Newcastle looking for sausages and fags, their behaviour demonstrates an early example of social interaction, when they would team up with a Fathasaurus in order to fuck in a hapless biffasaurus.

5 *Unkuldekkasaurus* This was a slow, lumbering beast characterised by dense bony thickening on the forehead, enabling it to serve a Byker teacake on other species. It also had large bony plates running the length of its spine, although arachaeologists are divided as to their purpose. Some say they acted like radiators, helping regulate blood tempurature, whilst others believe they were to attract the attention of other dinosaurs to allow the unkuldekkasaurus to ask them what the fuck they were looking at.

AARON A. AARDVARK

Incompetent Domestic Builder

★DRAINS CRACKED ★ CARPETS RUINED ★ CEMENT MIXED ON YOUR PATIO

All prices include 6 bags of hardened cement left by your front door. Plaster trailed through your home at no extra cost!

TEL: (0191) 233 002

Aaron A. Aardvark - not very good, but first in the book

Have-a-Go Builders
Established 1996
For a complete building service

BRICKWORK? PLASTERING? ROOFING? GLAZING? PLUMBING?

WE'LL HAVE A SHOT AT THE LOT!

ALL WORK UNDERTAKEN BY UNSKILLED BUT ENTHUSIASTIC WORKERS

TEL: 0191 377 353

You've tried the best - now try the rest!

Dodgy Brothers

Dubious Building Services

Time served tradesmen plus a couple of blokes you don't want in your house.

All building work undertaken plus:
- Sex chat lines called in your absence.
- Underwear drawers rifled and lingerie stolen.
- Wife's bra put on head - **GUARANTEED!**
- Follow up dirty phone calls to your missus.

(0191) 212 001

■ INVISIBLE BROS. ■

Tired of waiting in for builders who turn up late? Then call us and go out, because we don't turn up **at all**. No explanations. Nothing.

INVISIBLE BROS. Domestic Builders.

Specialists in:
★ Not turning up

Tel (0191) 469 790

For specialists in unpredictable hours and unexplained absences for weeks on end call

SPORADIC BUILDING SERVICES

We offer a range of services from puncturing the gas main on Christmas Eve to flooding your bathroom with shit and going on holiday for a month

All work guaranteed til we've been paid

Ask about:
- JOBS LEFT HALF FINISHED
- CARS BLOCKED IN BY SKIPS FOR WEEKS ON END
- UNTILED ROOFS POLYTHENED OVER THROUGHOUT WINTER
- WILDLY OPTIMISTIC ESTIMATES OF HOW LONG IT WILL TAKE

Slight drizzle? NO PROBLEM. We're off home.

For unreliable service at imaginative prices ring
0191 377 353

SEXIST BUILDERS LTD. Est. 1952

Complete Domestic Harrassment Specialists

*WOLF WHISTLES *SUGGESTIVE COMMENTS *LEERING *OPTIMISTIC PASSES AT HOUSEWIVES *SWEARING *OBSCENE GESTURES

A company with 44 years in the trade. Our craftsmen have Dagenham Smiles second to none and use only the foulest language in front of your children and neighbours

Call (0191) 416 790

■ RELUCTANT REPAIRS ■

Building & Roofing Repairs All jobs too large or too small

Call now for a fuck off price

Tel (0191) 377 353
(ansaphone)

Buffalo Billding Services, 104 Shit Street   Tyneside 0191 233 002

■ ROBDOG & SON ■

Overpriced Property Repair Service

Give us a call and kiss your savings goodbye.

The price we say is the price you pay - *and the fucking rest*

Tel. (0191) 377 353

Two Hoots Contractors

Boorish, ill-manered builders.

- Prompt, efficient service
- Gardens laid waste by boots
- Gallons of your tea demanded
- Very loud Radio One all day
- Polite requests acknowledged and completely ignored

Tel. (0191) 284 349

Remember- we ALWAYS pay the scantest regard to your property

Jack Churchill
& Son

A name you can trust - that's why I picked it.

For all your discouraging behaviour requirements.

Specialists in

★ TUTTING ★ SIGHING
★ PUSHING BACK HAT
★ SCRATCHING HEAD
★ SUCKING TEETH ★ WINCING

Tel. (0191) 233 002

■ NOT IN BUILDERS ■

For extensions, dormer windows, loft conversions - don't call us now, we're not in.

Tel. (0191) 212001

Sweaty Arsed Builders,
102 Hairy Knacker Street....**0191 377 353**

WHO DID THAT? BUILDERS

SPECIALISTS IN CRITICISING PREVIOUS BUILDING WORK

✳ *Others builders slagged off*
✳ *Your D.I.Y. laughed at*
✳ *Over reaction guaranteed*

We're also experts in prognostications of doom

Tel. 0191 284 349

Ne'er Do Well Builders,
103 Hairy Knacker Street....**0191 377 353**

Served Time Tradesmen Ltd.

The local builders you really can't trust

Specialists in

★ Stealing your lead flashing
★ Mysterious and arbitrary additional pricing systems
★ Things going missing

Call: (0191) 212 001

All quotations are likely to change depending on how much we think we can get from you. Fantastic prices for OAP's living alone.

■ BARELY-ADEQUATE LTD.■

Reasonable quality building work but nothing to sing about.

Tel. (0191) 284 349

For service with a 'Nile' it's got to be...

Wilson, Kepple & Betty
Est. 4000BC

Traditional Egyptian builders

For a full service in sphinx and pyramid erection. No job too colossal.

- HIEROGLYPHIC PLANS DRAWN UP
- LABOURERS ENTOMBED
- CURSES BESTOWED

Call us now and we'll be round in the morning with 10,000 slaves to give you an estimate.

From papyrus to topping out in six generations or your money back - no quibbles.

Call Tyneside (0191) 284 349
and ask for Amenhotep III

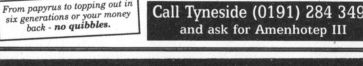

You Get What You Pay For With

KOST KUT KONSTRUCTORS

Specialists in all domestic building work done on the cheap.

All work done comes with our 25 year worthless guarantee

Brickwork-Joinery-Plumbing-Roofing

*Building regulations? - *fuck 'em*
*Poor quality materials used
*All responsibilities shirked

We have NO INSURANCE OVERHEADS!

Ring (0191) 233 002
We work to a price, not to a standard

15

CLAIM 3 ISSUES FOR £1 AND GET A REGULAR DOSE OF ADULT HUMOUR

Claim 3 issues of "Britain's Funniest Magazine" (manufacturers estimate) for just £1 today and get the best adult humour, featuring Viz's renowned characters such as the Fat Slags, Biffa Bacon and Roger Mellie, delivered FREE to your door.

Every issue of VIZ features:
- The world famous Viz letters page to really expand your mind
- Viz's unbeatable top tips
- Plenty of poor quality jokes
- Comic strips featuring all, well some, of your favourite characters
- Roger Mellie's updated Profanisaurus page – the ever expanding dictionary you can swear by
- And much more…

Claim 3 issues of VIZ for £1 today, and find out for yourself!
If during your 3 trial issues, you decide VIZ isn't for you, simply cancel and you won't pay a penny more. Best of all, if you continue reading you'll SAVE 26% on the shop price.

CALL NOW 0844 844 0380

HURRY!
Order online at: **www.dennismags.co.uk/viz**
CALL 0844 844 0380
using offer code G0812BKZ

---

 3 ISSUES FOR £1 OFFER

☐ **YES!** Please start my subscription to Viz with 3 issues for £1

To keep receiving VIZ, I don't have to do anything – my subscription will automatically continue at the LOW RATE of £10.99 every 5 issues (SAVING 26% on the shop price). I understand that if I'm not completely satisfied with VIZ, I can write to cancel during my trial period and I won't pay any more than the £1 already debited. The 3 issues for £1 are mine to keep, whatever I decide.

YOUR DETAILS

MR/MRS/MS/MISS   FORENAME

SURNAME

ADDRESS

POSTCODE   YEAR OF BIRTH

DAYTIME PHONE

MOBILE

EMAIL

Dennis Publishing reserves the right to limit this introductory offer to one per household.
You will be able to view your subscription details at www.subsinfo.co.uk

☐ **Direct Debit** 3 for £1, then £10.99 every 5 issues - **SAVE 26%** (UK only)

Dennis **Instruction to your Bank or Building Society to pay by Direct Debit** DIRECT Debit

Please complete and send to: Freepost RLZS-ETGT-BCZR, Dennis Publishing Ltd, 800 Guillat Ave, Kent Science Park, Sittingbourne ME9 8GU
Name and full postal address of your Bank or Building Society

To the manager: Bank name

Address

Postcode

Account in the name(s) of

Branch sort code

Bank/Building Society account number

Originator's Identification Number

7	2	4	6	8	0

Ref no. to be completed by Dennis Publishing

Instructions to your bank or Building Society
Please pay Dennis Publishing Ltd. Direct Debits from the account detailed in this instruction subject to the safeguards assured by the Direct Debit Guarantee. I understand that this instruction may remain with Dennis Publishing Ltd and, if so, details will be passed electronically to my Bank/Building Society.

Signature(s)

Date

Banks and building societies may not accept Direct Debit instructions for some types of account

Your details will be processed by Dennis Publishing Ltd (publishers of *Viz* magazine) and our suppliers in full accordance with UK data protection legislation. Dennis Publishing Ltd may contact you with information about our other products and services. Please tick if you prefer NOT to receive such information by post ☐ email ☐ phone ☐ mobile phone messaging ☐. Dennis Publishing Ltd occasionally shares data, on a secure basis, with other reputable companies that wish to contact you with information about their products and services. Please tick if you prefer NOT to receive such information by post ☐ phone ☐. Please tick if you DO wish to receive such information by email ☐ mobile phone messaging ☐. If the recipient of this subscription is under 18 please tick here ☐.

Return to: Freepost RLZS-ETGT-BCZR,
Viz subscriptions, 800 Guillat Avenue, Kent Science Park, Sittingbourne ME9 8GU

Offer Code: G0812B

In the editing suite of FTV studios where Roger's show *Fuck a Duck* is recorded. "I'm a professional. I don't do rehearsals."

Roger Mellie

It's hard to believe it's 35 years since my first broadcast as a cub reporter on the News with Robert Dougall. After all that time you'd think that my routine would be pretty well established by now. Let me tell you, it's not!

Following my wife's death last year I seem to be busier than ever sorting out the formalities. There seems to be no end of red tape involved at such a difficult time. Only last night I was up until the early hours with my lawyer, trying to block an exhumation order from the local CID. But life goes on.

I'm tremendously happy with my new partner, Candy (Candy Wonderbra- an 18-year-old researcher at Mellie's production company). She moved in shortly after my wife's death. Our relationship was purely platonic at first. She helped me to cope with all those complex feelings of loss, bereavement and isolation. However almost imperceptibly we found ourselves being drawn together, and by the time forensics had taken the body out of the bedroom, I had already given her one on the kitchen table. She's all a man could want - she's a wonderful cook, doesn't mind pushing the hoover about, and has absolutely no gag reflex.

I'm tremendously excited about my new gameshow (Fuck a Duck - weekdays 9.30 am BBC1). It's a bit like Catchphrase, but with general knowledge questions. You get fifty quid for every one you get right. If you get three in a row we bring out the ducks and then it really starts getting interesting. The animal rights protesters have been up in arms but it's just a bit of fun.

Rehearsals start at 10 a.m. but I've never been much of a morning person, so I tend to get out of bed some time in the early afternoon. There's an awful lot of standing around in studios doing fuck all involved

in television, and at my time of life I can do without it. Anyway, I'm a professional, I don't need to rehearse. The public like the occasional ad-lib or fluffed line. That bit where the elephant shat all over Val Singleton - was that scripted? Was it bollocks. Same when they carried Norman Tebbit out of that hotel in his jim-jams. Completely off the cuff - and it made great television.

I get to the studio round about 5.20. Shooting starts at 5.30, so there's time for a swift couple or three with Bob Holness in the bar before I go on. Half an hour later, the show's in the can and I'm back propping up the bar. Once the Six O'clock News is finished, Moira Stuart comes sprinting in for a drink and a go on the bandit. You could set your watch by her. I don't hang around much after then. After eight pints of Bass she's on the karaoke doing Unchained Melody, and it's time to leave.

Me and a few friends, (Alex Higgins, George Best and Chris Quinten) have just opened a restaurant in Stoke Newington, so I might pop in there for a few drinks before dinner. We've got a sort of nazi monkey theme, with the waitresses in gorilla costumes and swastika armbands. It's early days yet, and things are still a bit slow but we've all sunk a lot of money into this project so it's got to be a success.

I eat out most nights, but on my rare nights in it's not unknown for me to knock up a little something in the kitchen. I cook a mean Pasta 'n' Sauce, which I wash down with two or three bottles of sherry, before

heading out to the pub.

In my younger days I used to drink and drive without a second thought, but following my big accident (Mellie ran over and killed a bus queue in 1986) I am much more aware of how precious my licence is. These days if I've had a skinful, I drive very slowly and close to the kerb.

The pubs chuck out at half eleven, but the night is still young as far as I'm concerned. I head for my favourite club, an exclusive lap-dancing establishment in Acton, where I might stay until two or three in the morning. I've been down all the usual showbiz paths - sports cars, houses, drugs - but in a business where you can make ten grand cash for opening some poxy supermarket, I don't know any better way of spending money than stuffing it down some fat-titted bird's knickers.

One of the things I most regret is not having any kids. At least, none that I have access to. That's why I take very seriously my responsibilities as godfather to my producer Tom's young son (Tom jnr - aged 8). I try to pop round there five or six nights a week for a snack, a bit of a drink and to use his toilet on my way back from Acton.

I've been working with Tom now for fifteen years or more, and I've recently begun to notice how tired and stressed he's looking. I've seen the showbiz lifestyle do that to a lot of people around me. But I give him that same bit of advice that Robert Dougall gave me on the night of my first broadcast all those years ago: "It's not fucking brain surgery, Roger. It's just telly. Bollocks to it. Bollocks to everything."

Roger Mellie was talking to Parsley d'Lion.
NEXT WEEK: Rostrum cameraman Ken Morse.

157

Where's Wally's Rizlas?

Balthazar the house Christian has hidden five packets of Rizlas to stop Wally 'skinning up' some 'squidgy black', which he 'scored' at Glastonbury and brought back up his arse. There's a million pounds to be won if you find them all and simultaneously buy a winning lottery ticket.

160